Series / Number 01-060

Transitions to Stable Authoritarian-Corporate Regimes: The Chilean Case?

ROBERT R. KAUFMAN

Douglass College,
Rutgers University

⑤ SAGE PUBLICATIONS / Beverly Hills / London

For information address:

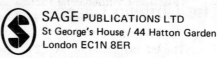

SAGE PUBLICATIONS, INC.
275 South Beverly Drive
Beverly Hills, California 90212

SAGE PUBLICATIONS LTD
St George's House / 44 Hatton Garden
London EC1N 8ER

International Standard Book Number 0-8039-0638-2

Library of Congress Catalog Card No. L.C. 75-38315

FIRST PRINTING

When citing a professional paper, please use the proper form. Remember to cite the correct Sage Professional Paper series title and include the paper number. One of the two following formats can be adapted (depending on the style manual used):

(1) NAMENWIRTH, J. Z. and LASSWELL, H. D. (1970) "The Changing Language of American Values." Sage Professional Papers in Comparative Politics, 1, 01-001. Beverly Hills and London: Sage Pubns.

OR

(2) Namenwirth, J. Zvi and Lasswell, Harold D. 1970. *The Changing Language of American Values.* Sage Professional Papers in Comparative Politics, vol. 1, series no. 01-001. Beverly Hills and London: Sage Publications.

CONTENTS

ROBERT R. KAUFMAN, Associate Professor of Political Science at Douglass College, Rutgers University, received his Ph.D. from Harvard University. Dr. Kaufman is the author of Politics of Land Reform in Chile *and articles on clientelism and dependency, published in* Comparative Studies in Society and History *and in* Comparative Politics. *He is presently at work on a comparative study of industrialization and authoritarianism in Argentina, Brazil, Chile, Mexico, and Uruguay.*

Transitions to Stable Authoritarian-Corporate Regimes: The Chilean Case?

ROBERT R. KAUFMAN
Douglass College,
Rutgers University

INTRODUCTION

Those who represent a political sector or a determined class will serve no one. This is a movement of a national and popular character [Augusto Pinochet, Commander-in-Chief of the Army].

We do not consider parties decisive for the progress of the country. Our line is one of total political transcendence. Our policy will be nationalistic, with participation of tecnicos, of youth organizations, of women, and naturally we will ignore their partisan allegiances when their specialties require it. We are not going to govern with parties [Air Force General Gustavo Leigh].

Chile has crossed . . . a Lircay which we trust will be decisive for her destiny as a free nation. Now, as then, the spirit of Portales inspires and vitalizes the reconstruction. And, in the present as in the past, the great mission is one of constructing a new juridical order, indigenous and stable, which channels without deviation the progress of this strong and virile people toward the future it deserves [Admiral José Toribio Merino].

We want a modern, flexible Constitution, which gives participation to women, which gives participation to gremios, which gives participation to youth; in which parliamentary offices are of a national character [Gustavo Leigh].

The Chilean military coup of September 1973 has reduced discussion of the possibilities of a "peaceful transition to socialism" in that country to a speculative debate over "might have beens." The coup also seems to have ended, perhaps for all time, Chile's happy status as a "deviant case" in

Latin America—a country which, in spite of profound social inequalities, possessed a seemingly stable and highly competitive constitutional order. If Chile does return to electoral politics, it is unlikely to be characterized by the openness and toleration which permitted the parties of Allende, Frei, and Alessandri to compete freely within the same legal framework. The infinitely more probable aftermath of a military withdrawal would be the kind of stalemated praetorianism suffered by Argentina after the fall of the first Perón regime: an alternation in office of weak civilian and military governments, each without the capacity to rule effectively because a large, alienated, and well-organized minority is denied the opportunity for meaningful political participation.

But for the present, the plans of the current junta do not seem to include an attempted return to old-style party politics of any sort. The Marxist parties have been outlawed; the others are "in recess"; and the Congress is "suspended." Echoing their military counterparts in Brazil and Peru, junta leaders speak vaguely of a "new order" in which the armed forces would have a permanent role, partisan allegiances would be "transcended," and functional associations of women, laborers, professionals, and businessmen would achieve direct representation within the decision-making organs of the state (*El Mercurio*, 1973). Thus far, it should be noted, such rhetoric has not been translated into concerted attempts to construct new institutional structures. The junta has appointed a commission of conservative jurists to draft a new constitution; but its primary energies have been focused on the more immediate tasks of eliminating leftist opposition, consolidating control over government, and establishing minimal social and economic stability. As a long-term objective, however, Chile's military leaders seem to be groping toward a form of rule that bears many of the features of what can be called an "authoritarian-corporate regime." A country which has already seriously experimented with both "moderate reform" and "peaceful socialist revolution" thus seems about to be launched on still another political experiment.

This paper examines the prospects for the "success" of such an authoritarian-corporatist experiment in Chile. Given a land where so many other political formulae have been debated and tried, and a contemporary situation which remains fluid and uncertain, such an examination must necessarily be speculative and inconclusive. It is impossible to predict with certainty whether Child will follow the "Argentine" or "Brazilian" road. The strategy followed here, therefore, is a more modest one. The first part of the paper presents a rough comparative framework which inventories and organizes the factors that seem to have promoted the consolidation of authoritarian-corporate regimes in other parts of Latin America and Mediterranean Europe; the second part of the paper synthesizes the available secondary literature on Chile and evaluates it in light of this comparative framework. The result of this exercise, hopefully, will be a better understanding of what we do and do not know about the crosscurrents at work in the specific Chilean situation and about the genesis of stable authoritarian-corporate systems elsewhere in the area.

I. A COMPARATIVE PERSPECTIVE

"Authoritarianism" is defined here as political rule on behalf of an unaccountable coalition of social and institutional elites. Authoritarian regimes, according to Juan Linz' (1964: 252-283) ideal-typical definition, have a hierarchical "mentality," but lack a defined, chiliastic ideology. They are tolerant of factional struggle and of a degree of competition among institutional interests; but they do not depend on periodic, competitive elections to legitimate their rule, and they do not permit an organized "loyal opposition" to seriously criticize or challenge their incumbency. Typically, they are also characterized by a party or parties subordinated to the state bureaucracy, by low levels of political mobilization, and by the predominance of the military establishment as a pillar of governmental authority.

"Corporatism"—a term roughly synonomous with Linz' (1964) concept of limited pluralism—refers to a pattern of state-group relationships in which formally organized, noncompetitive, officially-sanctioned functional associations monopolize interest representation and in turn are supervised by agents of the state bureaucracy (see Schmitter, 1974: 93-94). In ideal-typical terms, corporatist systems are vertically segmented societies, encapsulating individuals within a network or legally-defined guilds and corporations which derive their legitimacy from and in turn are integrated by a dominant bureaucratic center.

Authoritarianism and corporatism can occur separately in the empirical world and frequently do. Taken together, however, these concepts can be used to define an analytically distinct type of "developed" polity (thus, the term "authoritarian-corporate regime"), different in quality rather than degree from the "totalitarian" and "pluralist" models used so frequently in the political science literature. The pluralist response to the political challenges of economic development and social differentiation is to deconcentrate power and expand participation; the revolutionary socialist and fascist response is to organize participation through a dominant, ideological mass party. Authoritarian-corporate regimes employ corporatist controls to organize the interaction between the citizen and the state within an essentially autocratic framework. If the central problem of political development is, as Huntington (1968) suggests, to organize political participation within an increasingly modernized social context, then it is at least an arguable proposition that authoritarian-corporate rule constitutes a viable (if not desirable) pathway into the politically modern world (see Schmitter, 1972).

Notwithstanding the theoretical plausibility of this argument, however, concrete examples of stable authoritarian-corporate regimes are rare among countries with relatively "advanced" socioeconomic systems. The Soviet Union and the countries of Eastern Europe are perhaps evolving in this direction, but only after having gone through a prolonged period of revolutionary transformation and "totalitarian rule" (see Janos, 1970; Croan, 1970). The polities of North Africa and parts of Asia also have authoritarian-corporatist characteristics, but within relatively backward socioeconomic settings. Among the partially-industrialized states of Mediterranean Europe and Latin America, only Mexico—with its unique revolutionary background—provides a clear-cut example of a highly durable authoritarian-corporatist system. The contemporary regimes in Brazil and Peru have not yet demonstrated the capacity to survive over an extended period of time, but they do seem, for now, to be relatively well-entrenched and stable. Spain, prewar Italy, and Portugal can also be taken as examples of relatively durable authoritarian-corporatist systems, although recent events in the last-named country demonstrate how rapidly such regimes can disintegrate, even after many generations of political rule.

In spite of the problematic character of authoritarian-corporatist "pathways into political modernity," we lack clearly articulated hypotheses about the consolidation of such regimes. Theories of stable democracy and theories of revolution abound in the political science literature, but there is not to my knowledge a "theory of stable authoritarianism" that can provide the analytical guidelines for an examination of the Chilean case. It is not necessary, however, to begin this task completely from scratch. The study of Latin American politics has in recent years produced a growing body of literature on "authoritarianism" and "corporatism" which, though still highly speculative, does provide some useful arguments about the conditions which foster these phenomena. Information on specific countries which have undergone successful transitions—most notably, Spain, Portugal, Italy, Brazil, and Peru[1]—furnishes still another basis for generalization. Drawing on both types of sources, I have constructed a rough general framework for the analysis of the genesis and consolidation of authoritarian-corporate regimes, which can be applied to the Chilean case as well as, hopefully, to others.

SOME GENERAL COMMENTS ON THE FRAMEWORK

The primary purpose of the framework is to provide a relatively comprehensive summary of the general explanations of authoritarian-corporate rule. Many such explanations are vague, and some may eventually have to be revised beyond current recognition or discarded entirely. Since they are for the most part complementary rather than mutually exclusive, however, there is no preliminary need to choose between them; and in view of the early stage of the literature on authoritarian regimes, I have opted to include all arguments and propositions that seem plausibly linked to the final outcome.

A second purpose of the framework is to structure the various arguments and factors into four broader categories of explanation, depicted in Figure 1. The first category *(historical-environmental)* stresses factors "outside the boundaries" of the political system proper—the legacy of the country's past and aspects of its socioeconomic development. Under this rubric are the "medieval Catholic" heritage, delayed industrialization, and external dependency. The second category *(pre-authoritarian regime)* focuses primarily on the political-institutional patterns which, in the decades immediately preceding the transition to authoritarian-corporate rule, facilitate the success of that transition. The last two categories (the "triggering crisis" and the "international context") list the domestic and foreign situational factors which encourage a fundamental redefinition of the rules of the political game.

Finally, although the framework presented in Figure 1 is very far from a full-blown "theory," it does imply some assumptions about the way in which the various factors relate to one another and to the final outcome. These assumptions may be summarized as follows:

(1) The four categories of factors move successively from relatively distant to more proximate "causes" or authoritarian-corporate rule. The more "remote" historical-environmental factors produce an "elective affinity" for this type of rule, but by no means produce it in a strictly deterministic sense. Much of the impact of these factors, rather, is mediated through the political-institutional features of the pre-authoritarian regime, which provide a variety of structural conditions for a successful transition. The "crisis" and "international" factors, finally, provide the most direct incentives and resources for the final choices that produce authoritarian-corporate rule.

(2) Although the factors are loosely interrelated (as indicated by the arrows drawn in Figure 1) they can operate independently and in offsetting

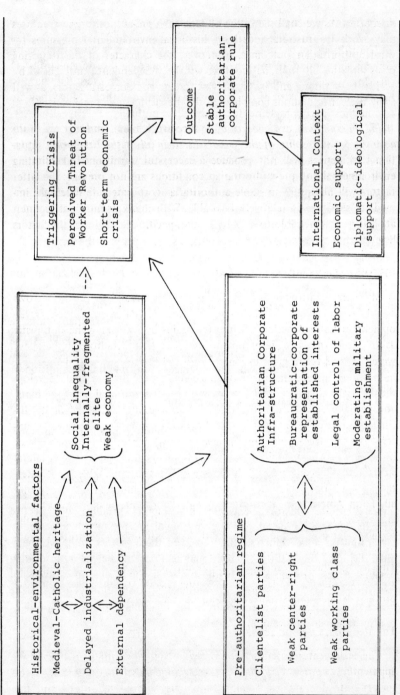

Figure 1

directions. As we shall see in the Chilean case, pre-authoritarian structures may work to frustrate underlying historical-environmental pressures toward authoritarian outcomes. Moreover, the character of the triggering crisis and the international context will be independently influenced by accidents of timing and by choices of foreign and domestic actors, as well as by the contradictions contained in the pre-authoritarian regime itself.

(3) A complete explanation of a successful transition must take into account at least some of the factors listed in all of the categories. Situational influences will not produce a successful transition, if facilitating environmental and pre-authoritarian conditions are not present; the latter factors will not result in stable authoritarian-corporate rule unless the immediate situation is relatively favorable. With these assumptions enumerated, it is now possible to turn to a more specific discussion of the factors listed within each category.

HISTORICAL-ENVIRONMENTAL FACTORS

My consideration of the factors presented under this rubric borrows heavily from Philippe Schmitter's (1972) essay, "Paths to Political Development in Latin America." Schmitter begins by criticizing the optimistic assumptions of early development theorists that "traditional societies" were destined to progress in direct linear fashion toward mass democracy; he proposes instead the utility of conceiving several ideal-typical "developmental tracks," which "depart from different traditional starting points, and perhaps arrive at equally stable but structurally and behaviorally distinct versions of the modern polity." Although movement of a given country from one track to another is always a possibility, "the probability of horizontal movement (along one path) is significantly greater than lateral shifts into adjacent paths." In an argument also applicable to Mediterranean countries, Schmitter suggests that most (although not necessarily all) Latin American nations move along a "corporate-authoritarian track" characterized by limits on political participation, a perpetuation of the social power of traditional elites, and the continuing concentration of political power within a central state bureaucracy (Schmitter, 1972: 88-93). The forces which allegedly encourage this pattern have been mentioned above: the medieval, Catholic "starting point" of this developmental process; delayed industrialization; and external dependence.

The Medieval, Catholic Tradition

The main feature of this tradition is an ongoing synthesis between two apparently contradictory legal-political principles: the organization of society into hierarchical, semi-autonomous "corporate" units; and the juridical concept that these units exist and are legitimated through the grace of a single, "patrimonial" center, which acts as an integrating and balancing force for the society as a whole (see Morse, 1973; Wiarda, 1973; Newton, 1973). Elements of this tradition can be traced as far back as the late Roman empire and have persisted in varying degrees throughout much of Europe. Its main principles, however, were particularly well-entrenched in the Mediterranean heartland of the empire, and most of all in the Iberian peninsula where the patrimonial concept of royal authority was reinforced by centuries of struggle with Islam. As a consequence, neither Mediterranean Europe nor its Latin American spin-off fully experienced the fuedal decentralization which in Northern and Western Europe helped to lay the basis for contractual theories of political obligation or for legal limitations on the power of the state. Nor, ironically, did the medieval synthesis allow for the rise of the kind of royal absolutism which elsewhere attempted to demolish the bastions of corporate privilege and to place citizens on an equal footing before the law. Society, as Richard Morse (1973: 67) has argued, was perceived as "composed of parts which relate through a patrimonial and symbolic center rather than directly to one another."

Writers who emphasize such cultural factors are often vague about the way they have influenced nineteenth and twentieth century political development in Southern Europe and Latin America. They do not, as a rule, try to explain how medieval Catholic patterns are transmitted over time, or why these patterns are more visible in some historical periods than in others. And they do not deal extensively with the implications of authoritarian-corporate tendencies outside the Mediterranean-Latin culture area. Nevertheless, it is not unreasonable to assume that such a deeply entrenched historical legacy does have some impact in Mediterranean and Latin countries. In many of them, "corporatist" and "patrimonial" principles have been stressed in the universities and law faculties, by *pensadores* and jurists, and in assorted legal codes and practices. Elites who are socialized within this framework might well be expected to be predisposed to react in "corporate" and "authoritarian" ways to the challenges of twentieth century modernization. And as a working hypothesis, if not as a demonstrated fact, these predispositions can plausibly account for at least some of the sociopolitical tendencies characteristic of development in Latin America and Southern Europe: the growth of the state bureaucracy as a source of protection and privilege for the upper and middle classes; the creation of "official" unions which co-opt or coerce the emergent labor movement; and the tendency for both civilian strongmen and military establishments to claim an "apolitical" moderating and integrating role strikingly similar to that performed by the earlier monarchy.

Delayed Industrialization

This concept contrasts the characteristics of late nineteenth and twentieth century industrialization in Latin America and Southern Europe with
two prior "waves" of industrialization occurring in the North Atlantic
countries and Western Europe (see Hirschman, 1971; O'Donnell, 1974;
Kurth, 1973; Gerschenkron, 1962; Collier, 1975). In the first wave, especially in Britain, the export of manufactured textiles and other consumer
goods played a central role. The second "wave" (Germany, France, Swe-
den, Russia) was characterized by a sudden "spurt" in the manufacture of
capital goods, produced for export or for military purposes. The "very
late" industrializers of Southern Europe and Latin America, finally, tended
to emphasize import-substitution industrialization, starting "with relatively
small plants administering 'last touches' to a host of imported [consumers]
goods" and only later moving into the production of capital inputs (Hirschman, 1971: 95). This process tended to lack the "convulsive elan" of second wave countries; and though the emphasis on consumer goods resem-
bled that of the first wave, the Mediterranean and Latin countries did not
undergo the long, evolutionary process of social transformation and learn-
ing which preceded the first industrial revolution, and lacked the export
possibilities of the earlier industrializers.

As in much of the literature on "modernization," there is much that
remains to be refined conceptually and demonstrated empircally in this set
of contrasts. To the extent that they are historically valid, however, they
suggest a number of important implications for the prospects of authoritarian-corporate rule.

In the first place, in all but the earliest wave, industrialization was as
much a public as a private enterprise—one which tended to strengthen the
power both of the state and of the traditional elites. "Backwardness"
created strong incentives for state direction of industrialization; for the
formation of industrial cartels; and for a close integration between the
government bureaucracy, landowners, and the industrial elite. In the "very
late" Mediterranean and Latin cases, moreover, the industrialists lacked
the political prestige of their earlier, export-oriented counterparts and this,
according to Kurth (1973: 28), made them "especially willing to maintain
the power of the agricultural elites, to accept their demands, and to merge
the parties of the two."

Second, by the late nineteenth and early twentieth centuries, the international diffusion of labor organizations created a different domestic context for societies in the process of industrialization. On the one hand, it
produced a tendency for "premature" welfare and consumptionist demands which threatened the process of capital accumulation. On the other,

it created strong tendencies toward governmental preemption and control of worker demands through the institution of "captive" labor organizations, tied to the state bureaucracy. In Mediterranean Europe, this was reflected in the wave of full-fledged, counterrevolutionary authoritarian-corporate regimes which were established in the wake of worker radicalism in the 1920s and 1930s. In Latin America, these pressures were initially expressed within a somewhat more benign "populist" experience, in which governmental and industrial elites attempted to win the positive support of the labor movement by tying welfare benefits to new corporate structures. In neither region, however, was the relatively weak industrial elite in a position to fundamentally challenge the agrarian oligarchy; and in both, there was an overriding common interest in establishing bureaucratic controls which might prevent the emergence of a genuinely independent and powerful labor movement.

Finally, although industrialization in the Mediterranean and Latin countries increased the importance of the urban manufacturing sector, it did not—like earlier experiences—furnish a strong impulse for overall social transformation or economic expansion. Manufacturing for existing domestic markets did not initially require major changes in the productive or social relations in the other economic sectors; as a consequence, industrial expansion ultimately tended to generate erratic growth and "bottlenecks," rather than "take-offs." Especially in the Latin American cases, import-substitution involved a continuing dependence on raw material exports, increasing external debt to pay for capital imports, an overstaffed public bureaucracy, protected inefficient industrial oligopolies, and a relatively slow growth of employment opportunities within the industrial sector—all conducive to extreme social tensions and to the imposition of authoritarian rule.

External Dependence

This in my judgment has both the most ambiguous and the most intriguing theoretical connection with the emergence of authoritarian-corporate rule. Unquestionably the penetration of foreign capital into the countries of Southern Europe and Latin America, the vulnerability of these countries to world economic conditions, the incursions of foreign ideologies and governments, all have had important effects in specific cases—not the least of which is Chile. Yet the consolidation of the Spanish and Portuguese authoritarian-corporate regimes occurred in virtually autarkic economic contexts; and in several Latin American cases (notably in Mexico and Peru), nationalistic rhetoric and expropriation helped contribute to the entrenchment of their present political orders. The multifaceted consequences of external dependence thus require a more careful sorting out than is possible here. Nevertheless, external dependence does seem highly relevant to authoritarian outcomes in at least two general ways.

In the first place, it is obviously related closely to the phenomenon of delayed industrialization. Particularly in Latin American cases, the traditional dependence on raw material exports served to reinforce the dominance of a small, agro-commercial elite and to retard the growth of a domestic manufacturing sector. The subsequent import-substitution industrialization, moreover, actually increased economic dependence in many ways: increasing reliance on capital imports; expanding foreign debt; opening the way for foreign investment in the manufacturing sector; and leaving the economy as a whole vulnerable to the vicissitudes of the flow of international trade and credit (see Frank, 1967).

Second, it can be persuasively argued that external dependence contributes to authoritarian-corporate rule through its historic impact on the class structure of dependent nations. On the one hand, there is evidence that both the traditional forms of trade dependency and the newer forms of multinational penetration have encouraged and/or perpetuated highly stratified social structures, characterized by extreme concentrations of wealth and by the "marginalization" of the urban and rural poor (see Cutright, 1967; Tyler and Wogart, 1973; Kaufman, Geller, Chernotsky, 1975). In particular, the availability of foreign resources helps to smooth over the functional cleavages between agricultural, industrial, and commercial elites' and to reinforce their control over the rest of the society. At the same time, foreign penetration has also often encouraged severe intra-class rivalries, based not on functional differences but on different kinds of links to the world economic order. Competing foreign interests, for example, often generated mutually antagonistic domestic clienteles among the upper and middle sectors of Latin America and Southern Europe. Similarly, "cosmopolitan" elites, tied to the export trade, tended to conflict with those in the more isolated, interior regions. And, with the penetration of foreign capital into the industrial sector, white and blue-collar workers in the newer, more capital-intensive industries were set apart from those employed in the more traditional manufacturing branches and in the tertiary sector. By encouraging a social order with so many crisscrossing lines of cleavage, external dependency thus inhibits the formation of strong, class-based political associations and leads to the "sort of nationally stalemated, nonhegemonic class and interest structure which Karl Marx postulated as the distinctive basis for Bonapartism" (Schmitter, 1972: 101).

PRE-AUTHORITARIAN REGIMES

The impact of the historical-environmental factors outlined above will be mediated in part by the way they are organized and expressed in political-institutional terms. The "pre-authoritarian" category focuses precisely on such modes of political expression in countries such as Spain, Italy, Portugal, Brazil, and Peru in the decades just prior to the emergence of full-blown authoritarian-corporate regimes. How were the liberal-constitutional forms of such regimes superimposed upon the social structures of the countries in question? What conditions of the old regimes facilitated the transition to overt authoritarian-corporate rule?

In his study of Spain's "pre-authoritarian" party system, Juan Linz (1967: 198) provides an important part of the answer. In the Spanish constitutional monarchy of the restoration period:

> the "real country" was not or could not be mobilized and integrated into the "official country" created by the political class and its supporters. The [parliamentary system] was unable to assimilate some of the traditionalist opposition on the periphery, to use the talents of the growing industrial and commercial bourgeoisie, and to win the talents of the small but lively academic and nonacademic intelligentsia. The system was controlled by professional politicians, mostly lawyers, professionals, and landowners, who relied on the largely apolitical and even illiterate mass electorate of the countryside and the provincial cities and towns—populations often brought to the polls by local notables or bosses.

This metaphoric notion of a gap between the "real" and "official" countries highlights the main characteristic (and ultimately, one of the principal weaknesses) of pre-authoritarian regimes in general: in most, the internally-divided but socially "established" middle and upper class elites tended to bypass or oppose constitutional channels of political influence as means of defending their categorical interests.

An "official" constitutional apparatus of roles and processes did operate in these countries, as Linz suggests. Legislative and ministerial offices were filled by an active "political class" which specialized in the mobilization of electoral support. In the more stable countries of Western Europe and North America, however, these processes involved the organization of relatively well-differentiated political parties which, even before the rise of the workers' movements, channeled the interests of agrarian and industrial elites, of competing religious forces, and of the "center" and "periphery" into the constitutional arena (see Lipset and Rokkan, 1967). In the Mediterranean and Latin countries, general developmental forces produced a cleavage pattern which did not lend itself to the formation of well-defined party structures. Although individual "politicos" were often drawn from the upper classes, the parties they organized were loosely-structured, poorly-differentiated clientelistic affairs, representing only narrow, personal interests.

"Real" power, on the other hand, was exercised elsewhere in the system—through what might be called an authoritarian-corporate infrastructure. The central features of this infrastructure have already been implied in the preceding discussion: a civil bureaucracy which served as the primary arena for the representation of "established" interests; the economic weakness and state control of the lower classes; and a military establishment which claimed the role of a "neutral" arbiter and referee of the political game.

In view of these patterns, it should not be surprising that, even after many decades of apparent stability, the parliamentary forms of pre-authoritarian regimes tended to wither away quickly in the face of crises which accompanied socioeconomic "modernization." As antisystem, working class movements began to make use of the electoral arena, clientelist machines were in no position to compete effectively. To preserve their "social" power, as Marx (1959) put it, established elites found it necessary to relinquish their "political" power, exercised sparingly at best through representative institutions. For our purposes, however, the important point is that many of the same "pre-authoritarian" features which contributed to the collapse of the old order also facilitated the building of a new one. In this context, and as a prelude to the subsequent consideration of the Chilean case, the following pre-authoritarian conditions should be highlighted as being relevant to a successful transition.

Weakness of Prosystem Conservative and Moderate Parties

This corollary of clientelistic forms of electoral mobilization implies the absence of a potentially important obstacle to a successful transition. The "political class" of pre-authoritarian regimes, lacking organizational resources and a broad social base, formed no real impediment to the permanent elimination of electoral competition. In Brazil, the leading "politicos" were simply deprived of their "political rights," having no real means of resisting such measures. Or, they could be co-opted into subordinate roles within the new order—a pattern which occurred in Spain for example with the incorporation of Catholic centrists, monarchists, and Carlists into the framework of an already subordinated Falangist movement (see Linz, 1970). Such processes of exclusion or co-optation are presumptively more difficult in a country like Chile, where strong Christian Democratic and rightist parties existed prior to the coup—a point explored in more detail below.

The Centrality of the Civil Bureaucracy

This pattern, already alluded to above, provides an important ground of continuity between the old regime and the new one. The use of the bureaucracy as an arena of elite representation facilitated the transformation of these "established" social forces into "pillars" of an authoritarian-corporate order. The prior existence of bureaucratic-legal controls of working class activity provided, at the same time, a framework for the subordination of the traditional "targets" of authoritarian-corporate regimes (see Schmitter, 1971, 1973).

Weakness of the Working Class Movement

Although pre-authoritarian regimes usually crumbled before the *threat* of a workers' "revolution," both the character of economic change and the institution of bureaucratic controls tended to inhibit strong, independent working class organization. Even in the case of Spain, where Communists and Socialists led the loyalist resistance, the Spanish Socialist party did not become a major force until the mid-1930s, and the Communist were never able to acquire more than a small percentage of the total vote. In 1964 Brazil, the workers' movement (the PTB) was an unstructured populist mass which emerged without strong central leadership within a trade union structure that had long been manipulated by the state. Although the APRA party was considerably stronger in Peru, it had never been able to penetrate effectively into the urban slums or the sierra. In both the Mediterranean and the Latin cases, finally, there existed a large, political unattached rural mass which could be relatively easily mobilized or depoliticized to suit the interest of the new regime. This does not, of course, mean that a well-organized, militant workers' movement can never be repressed through authoritarian means—Mussolini and Hitler both proved the contrary. As a *ceteris paribus* proposition, however, it is likely that the success of an authoritarian-corporate transition will vary inversely with the degree of organization and the scope of support of lower class political movements.[2]

High Military "Governing Capacity"

The military's pre-authoritarian role as a "moderating" power seemed to prepare it in virtually all cases to act as the pivot for a successful transition to authoritarian-corporate rule. This factor, however, seems especially relevant to the regimes (Brazil and Peru) which consolidated in the 1960s. Although the military also played a pivotal role in the transitions of the

1930s and thus required a degree of cohesion and discipline, a personal caudillo—a Franco, Mussolini, or a Salazar—provided an effective personal center of authority. In Peru and Brazil, however, substantially more modernized social infrastructures had made possible the emergence of a far more professionalized military establishment, while the moderating roles performed by these establishments in the pre-authoritarian regime had equipped them with political skills well-suited to permanent and largely impersonal forms of authoritarian-corporate rule (Stepan, 1973). As a result, the Peruvian and Brazilian armed forces constitute an important point of comparison with the Chilean military establishment, which lacks many of these same qualities.

THE TRIGGERING CRISIS

Authoritarian-corporate regimes are brought into being through the catalyst of severe domestic crises. In some respects, it should be noted, these crises are the products of earlier political patterns, and difficult to distinguish from the pre-authoritarian regime as such. Yet the profound aggravation of earlier contradictions and abrupt changes in "politics-as-usual" are essential in providing significant new incentives for the development of new political structures. (How could Franco's Spain, for example, be understood without taking into account the trauma of the civil war?) Given the importance of such incentives and the uncertainty characteristic of transitional periods, the crisis situation deserves separate consideration as a factor influencing the consolidation of authoritarian-corporate rule.

Precisely because crises are "exceptional," they are difficult to analyze comparatively. Profound crises open the way for accidents of timing and for the choices and actions of domestic and foreign leaders to play decisive roles. Despite the difficulties in generalization, however, at least two sets of issues seem ubiquitous in triggering crises and provide a basis for some degree of generalization: one, already implied, is the threat perceived by established social and political forces as the result of accelerated attempts to mobilize the working class into "anti-system" political movements; the second is the aggravated inability of the pre-authoritarian system to cope with the economic problems of growth and inflation. A successful transition to authoritarian-corporatist rule seems to depend in large on the relative salience of these two issues and on the magnitude of the crisis which each provokes.

When mobilization threats are perceived as most salient, extreme crisis tends to drive together otherwise hostile and competing, "established" social forces and political factions. The mobilization of loyalist forces in Spain, for example, clearly prompted the Catalan bourgeoise, Castilians centralists, landowners, fascist intellectuals, monarchists, and Catholic conservatives to coalesce around the politically "neutral" army led by Franco. In Brazil in 1964, similarly, strong fear of the "socialist" tendencies unleashed by the Goulart government helped to override a multitude of regional and political anatagonisms between northeast landowners, coffee growers, industrialists of the southeast, small manufacturers, and salaried workers.

On the other hand, the "economic" dimension of the triggering crisis lacks such unifying effects and often tends to exacerbate differences between groups which are otherwise agreed on the desirability of excluding the "popular" sector from political participation. Solutions to the problems of growth and inflation impose upon authoritarian rulers the need for "hard" decisions that are almost certain to penalize at least some members of the supporting coalition. If these decisions do not yield quick results (in terms of economic growth and price stability) and/or if they are not offset by the fear of lower class revolution, the tension produced by the scramble for economic welfare are likely to increase the probability of opposition to the new government, to weaken the unity necessary to impose "reforms," and to jeopardize the prospects for political consolidation.

A brief reference to Ongania's aborted attempt to establish an authoritarian-corporate regime in Argentina should suffice to illustrate this point (O'Donnell, 1973: 102). Although part of the motive for this attempt was fear of the Peronist movement, the hostilities between the "establishment" and the increasingly conservative Peronist unions were already beginning to fade by the mid-1960s; and an equally, if not even more significant motivation for the attempt was the broad dissatisfaction with inflation and stagnation. But whatever the general consensus on the desirability of excluding the Peronists, there was no agreement on the policies designed to control the economic situation. Domestic entrepreneurs, white-collar workers, agrarian elites, and others, were clearly threatened by the antiinflationary measures imposed by the new military and civilian technocratic rulers. In Brazil, at about the same time, similar cleavages were counterbalanced by, among other things, the fresh memory of the just-deposed Goulart regime. In Argentina, however, less of a clear and present danger existed to offset the economic discontent of middle and upper sector groups. The resulting dissension within both established military and civilian sectors increased still further the difficulties of repressing an already strong Peronist movement and thus was among the contributing causes of the collapse of the Ongania government.

THE INTERNATIONAL CONTEXT

This category subsumes the diplomatic, economic, and military pressures emanating from a country's international environment at the time of its attempted transition to authoritarian-corporate rule. Along with the issues presented by the triggering crisis, these pressures embrace the situational determinants of a successful transition.

In a broader sense, of course, the international environment has already been built into the analysis at another important point in the general framework—in the discussion of external dependency and delayed industrialization. Moreover, in many individual cases, war and international depression have fed the pressures leading to the collapse of pre-authoritarian regimes and have shaped the mobilization and economic issues connected with the triggering crisis.

At this point, however, the "international context" category is intended to highlight the more direct impact that foreign attitudes and behaviors may have on the consolidation of authoritarian-corporate regimes. Such influences may be quite diffuse, as was the case with the general international "respectability" of corporatist ideologies during the 1930s—a respectability which in a broad way facilitated the legitimation of authoritarian rule in Spain, Portugal, Italy, and parts of Eastern Europe. Considerably more concrete influences may also be at work—the German military and financial support provided to Franco, for example, or the massive U.S. public and private aid which flowed to Brazil after 1964.

Although these kinds of influence, like the ones associated with the triggering crisis, are extremely difficult to abstract meaningfully from concrete temporal and spatial settings, the examination of at least two general factors seems warranted within a broad, comparative framework:

(1) High levels of ideological and diplomatic support available to new authoritarian-corporate regimes from powerful international actors.

(2) The availability of public and private economic aid for the new regime.

Such factors are unlikely to be sufficient explanations for the consolidation of authoritarian-corporate rule. In the absence of at least some "favorable" domestic conditions, even massive amounts of foreign support may be inadequate to prop up a tottering regime. Where developmental, institutional, and domestic situational factors work in different directions, however, foreign support may well be necessary to tip the outcome of an authoritarian enterprise one way or another. For this reason, even though the nature of this support cannot be more clearly specified in theoretical terms, it is too important to be ignored either in discussions of authoritarian-corporate rule in general or in the analysis of a single case such as Chile.

II. APPLICATION OF THE FRAMEWORK
TO THE CHILEAN CASE

In this part of the paper, the framework just elaborated will be used in three ways to analyze the prospects for the consolidation of authoritarian-corporate rule in Chile.

(1) The individual factors summarized above can be employed to iden-tify the forces in the Clilean case which facilitate or impede a successful transition. Although a detailed discussion of these forces must await further explication below, my own conclusions about the way they "match up" to the general framework are summarized in Table 1. As can be seen, they add up to a rather complex picture. In general, the historical-environ-mental factors which generally encourage authoritarian-corporate rule are present in the Chilean case. On the other hand, however, Chile lacks sev-eral important features of "typical" pre-authoritarian regimes. The factors associated with the triggering crisis and the international context are also mostly negative, although one of these factors—the widespread upper and middle class fear of a workers' revolution—does create a significant politi-cal resource for the current military regime. In short, as we move from one category of factors to the next, the forces at work in the Chilean case ap-pear increasingly ambiguous and contradictory.

TABLE 1

General factors contri-buting to a successful transition	Related Chilean conditions	Comments
I. Historical-environmental		
A. Med.-Catholic heritage	yes	
Delayed industrialization	yes	Initiated in 1920s
External dependency	yes	One of most dependent LA countries
B. Extreme social inequality	yes	Gini index of land and income inequality among the highest in Latin America
Weak economy	yes	Slow, erratic growth; chronic inflation
Internally-fragmented social elite	no	A major reason for early consolidation of consti-tutional government

TABLE 1 (Continued)

General factors contributing to a successful transition	Related Chilean conditions	Comments
II. Pre-authoritarian regime		
A. Clientelist parties		
Weak center and right parties	no	Socially and ideologically differentiated Radical, National, and Christian Democrat parties
Weak working class parties	no	Although some weaknesses, one of the most powerful in LA
B. Authoritarian-corporatist infrastructure		
Bureaucratic-corporate representation of established interests	yes	Began to erode seriously in the 1960s
Legal controls of labor	partial	Legislation passed in 1920s, but not as effective as elsewhere, because of party competition
Political preparedness of "moderating" military	no	However, some predispositions were present
III. Triggering crisis		
Perceived threat of "revolution"	yes	Extremely profound after Allende's election
Short-term economic crisis	no	Major economic collapse; recovery extremely difficult
IV. International context		
Economic support	no	
Diplomatic-ideological support	no	

(2) The second objective, to a large extent dictated by this mixed picture, is to trace at least some of the interconnections between the various factors as they appear in the Chilean case. The first of the ensuing sections thus explores the reasons why, in Chile, external dependence, delayed industrialization, and a medieval, Catholic heritage produced such atypical pre-authoritarian institutions, as well as some rather typical pressures for constitutional breakdown and authoritarian rule. The second focuses primarily on the way two of the most important atypical features of Chile's pre-authoritarian regime—a politically "unprepared" military and a highly organized working class movement—affect the prospects for long-term

authoritarian-corporate rule. The third and fourth sections explore aspects of the domestic and international situations in the context of these two previous perspectives. In other words, the framework is not simply "super-imposed" mechanically on top of the Chilean "reality," but is used in a more flexible way, as an exploratory tool which should help us understand, rather than blind us to, the configurative complexities of the case under study.

(3) The final objective is to hazard some guesses about the overall possibilities of authoritarian-corporate consolidation in Chile. Although this analysis is not intended primarily as a predictive exercise, the framework's application to the Chilean case does suggest some tentative projections into the short-run Chilean future. This is attempted in the brief "conclusion" at the end of the paper.

HISTORICAL-ENVIRONMENTAL FACTORS IN THE CHILEAN CASE

It is reasonably clear from most available evidence that the broad forces shaping Chilean development conform quite closely to the historical-environmental factors presented in the framework.

This is perhaps most apparent with respect to the "external dependence" factor. As early as the middle of the seventeenth century, the Chilean economy was geared to the export of wheat and minerals and (especially after the break with Spain) dependent on imported British manufactured goods and portfolio investment. In the 1880s a second important feature of Chilean dependency was added: the direct control by foreign companies of the export sector. From the 1880s until the collapse of the nitrate market in the 1920s, the nitrate-based export sector was dominated by British firms. Afterwards, until Allende expropriated them in 1972, American multinationals controlled the mining, refining, and marketing of Chilean cooper, a product which accounts for about 80 percent of Chilean foreign exchange earnings. As Chile began to industrialize during the second quarter of the twentieth century, foreign interests penetrated the service and manufacturing sector as well, controlling at least 50 percent of the production of machinery and equipment, iron and steel, petroleum products, chemicals and rubber, and automotive assembly (Cockroft et al., 1973: 13). By the 1960s, cross-sectional indicators suggested that Chile was one of the most dependent of the Latin American countries, ranking second in both the annual per capita flow of U.S. public and private investment and in the per capita value of accumulated foreign capital.[3]

The Chilean industrialization process, initiated in the 1920s and 1930s, was also almost a classic example of the delayed, import-substitution patterns described above. As balance of payments difficulties of the interwar years reduced Chile's import capacity, a variety of light industrial firms appeared on the scene, producing such items as paper and textiles for local consumption. This was followed in the 1940s and 1950s by the expansion of a capital goods industry (also producing for a domestic market) which was heavily subsidized and regulated by the state. Although this process did allow for the extension of jobs and some welfare benefits to an expanded white and blue-collar sector, it neither transformed the fundamentally hierarchical character of Chilean society nor furnished a particularly strong impetus for overall growth. As in most other cases, the principal benefit from industrialization went to an enlarged urban-rural oligarchy, while a large mass of peasants and lumpenproletarians bore most of the costs. Also quite typically, overall economic expansion was retarded by a variety of bottlenecks—an overextended welfare structure, low agricultural productivity, continued dependence on copper exports, a limited domestic market, and inefficient industrial oligopolies—all of which in the 1950s and 1960s produced both chronic unemployment and strong inflationary pressures (see Sunkel, 1965; Felix, 1961; Petras, 1969).

Finally, at least since the time of Diego Portales (the "founding father" of Chile's early nineteenth century republic), a Catholic, corporative, and usually conservative intellectual and legal tradition has appeared to play an important role in Chilean political life. The Conservative party—for a century the bellweather of the Chilean right—was quite clearly linked to this tradition, as were at least some sectors of the powerful Christian Democratic party. A number of writers have found significant Catholic legal influences in the Chilean constitutions of 1833 and 1925 and in the property and labor codes written in the 1920s (see Moreno, 1969; Morris, 1966; Howe, 1973). Finally, since 1973, the current junta has at times appeared to be strongly influenced by a small group of conservative intellectuals, based in the *Universidad Católica,* whose rhetoric closely parallels that of Falangist Spain.[4]

These forces would appear to locate Chile rather directly on an authoritarian-corporate developmental "track." From this perspective, it should not be particularly surprising that Chilean "democracy" eventually collapsed or that authoritarian "solutions," similar to those of other Latin and Mediterranean cases, were attempted. The more difficult analytical problem, especially from a comparative perspective, is to understand why the evolution toward pluralism got as far as it did, especially in the three decades preceding the overthrow of the Allende government. As we shall see, a variety of authoritarian tendencies did exist beneath the surface of Chilean constitutionalism all along, intertwined in various ways with the political-institutional structures of that country. Yet the Chilean pre-authoritarian regime *was* different. Between 1939 and 1973, relatively well-defined political parties competed more or less freely in a stable legislative-electoral arena; Marxist parties were allowed to operate more or less independently and to dominate a relatively militant and independent labor movement; and in the 1950s and 1960s, the mass base of the political system was gradually expanded to include virtually all strata of the Chilean population. The remainder of this section deals with this paradoxical relationship between polity and society. Why did Chilean constitutionalism emerge and consolidate within such an apparently inhospitable historical-environmental setting? How did authoritarian tendencies constrain this development prior to 1973? What are the implications of this contradictory developmental pattern for the ultimate consolidation of a full-blown authoritarian-corporate regime?

Historical-Environmental Factors and the Pre-Authoritarian Order

To understand the evolution of Chile's rather stable constitutional order, it is necessary to look more closely at the way in which our "historical-environmental" factors unfolded over time and interacted with existing political structures in the course of three phases of Chilean political development: the so-called autocratic republic (1833-1891); the parliamentary period (1891-1925); and the pre-authoritarian multiparty system itself, which took shape in the 1930s and 1940s and persisted until September 1973.

My principal argument (which admittedly requires considerably more in-depth and comparative research) can be summarized in three main points:

(1) In the early nineteenth century, certain aspects of Chilean dependency made possible an unusually easy consolidation of political authority, initially along autocratic lines that were consistent with the medieval, Catholic legacy;

(2) This early consolidation in turn paved the way for direct oligarchic parliamentary rule from 1891 to 1925, and for the development of Chilean political parties; and

(3) During the 1930s and 1940s, the prior development of a parliamentary arena provided an institutional matrix within which import-substitution policies could serve as a basis for the partial integration of middle and working class parties into the system.

An elaboration of the first point, concerning the character of Chilean dependency, requires a brief reference back to a broader comparative context. Among most of the newly established Latin American republics of the nineteenth century, foreign interests penetrated unevenly and often competitively into each society, and frequently provided an important stimulus for severe rivalries among segments of the domestic elite. In Argentina, for example, the externally-oriented oligarchy of Buenos Aires clashed repeatedly with the more parochial elites of the interior. In Mexico, to take another well-known instance, even more complex struggles occurred between the heirs of the old colonial trading monopolies, free-traders, and the domestic clienteles of competing British, U.S., French, and German interests. Once the restraining "patrimonial" mantle of the Spanish monarchy was discarded, similar conflicts occurred throughout the region, making it virtually impossible in most countries to institutionalize any legitimate form of political rulership.

Although Chile's preindustrial ties to the world economy were similar in most respects to those of her neighbors, these links had a different, less divisive impact on intra-elite relationships. Instead, the concentration of the Chilean population in the temperate central and south central regions, coupled with the relatively early participation of both regions in international wheat trade, produced a hacienda economy dominated by a relatively homogeneous, commercially-oriented agrarian oligarchy. After independence, this oligarchy could readily agree on the advantages of free trade with Britain; and through intermarriage and joint commercial ventures, it rather quickly developed close ties with the foreign and domestic merchant colonies springing up in Valparaiso. The more direct and potentially disruptive forms of foreign penetration, found so frequently elsewhere, did not come to Chile until the 1880s, with the acquisition of the northern mining territories and the formation of British-owned nitrate firms. It is from this period onward that one finds the more familiar patterns of Chilean dependency sketched out above. By this time, however, there had already emerged a well-consolidated, elite-based political order (see Pregger, 1975).

In the initial phases of this consolidation, another historical-environmental factor—the medieval, Catholic heritage—also entered the Chilean picture in an unusual way. Ironically, the very unity with which the Chilean upper classes opened the door to British economic influence allowed them to close it for almost a half century to the "subversive" parliamentary, federalist, and democratic slogans which reinforced elite conflicts elsewhere. Under the leadership of Portales, a Valparaiso merchant, the Chilean elite instead quite consciously accepted a conservative authority formula deemed more consistent with "authentic" Chilean traditions, one which recapitulated many of the structures and functions of the old Spanish monarchy (Collier, 1967; Morse, 1973: 57). Although the constitution of 1833 provided for a congress and for limited elections, Chile was effectively governed until the late 1800s by a succession of presidential "auto-crats," each legally selected for a ten-year period and each expected to use his substantial authority to moderate the relatively mild rivalries be-tween congressionally-based aristocratic factions.

Serious demands for legislative supremacy did begin to appear in the late nineteenth century, partly as the result of "liberal" pressures of new wealth emanating from the nitrate territories; and in 1891, Chile entered in-to a thirty-year period of political rule by a parliamentary oligarchy. By this time, however, Chile's unique blend of economic liberalism and political conservatism had institutionalized and unified the juridical order; and the "aristocracy" as a whole was ready, not only to incorporate the mining bourgeoisie into its ranks, but to insert itself directly into the polity through legislative forms. Portales, the "autocrat" whose spirit is so pas-sionately invoked by contemporary Chilean authoritarians, had thus helped indirectly to implant parliamentary institutions rather firmly in Chilean soil. Under his leadership, the typical sequences of many Latin American and Southern European states had been reversed: liberal consti-tutionalism was not inaugurated by a feeble "modernizing" elite in a new, divided nation, but through the collective action of a relatively united upper class, seeking to translate social power into political power by seizing the machinery of an already established state (see Kurth, 1973: 2-11).

It is not necessary to dwell extensively on the ensuing parliamentary period: its pivotal role in preparing the transition to a more broad-based multiparty system seems relatively self-evident. Two important features of this system seem worth underlining, however, before proceding to a dis-cussion of the pre-authoritarian regime itself.

In the first place, the institutionalization of parliamentary politics in the early part of the twentieth century contributed significantly, as Arturo Valenzuela (1975) points out, to the development of "pro-system" Chilean political parties. Because aristocratic factions were no longer able to turn to a strong president for the arbitration of disputes, they began in the classic British fashion to mobilize support outside of the parliamentary arena, largely through the activation of patron-client ties and the dispensa-tion of patronage to local political bosses. At least three of the major contemporary political parties—the Conservatives and Liberals (which in 1967 merged to form the National Party) and the Radicals—evolved initial-ly in this way. With the first two parties representing the interests of major economic elites and the latter coming to embrace a large range of the middle class, these party structures did much to link "established" social sectors to the pre-authoritarian constitutional order and to deter the for-mation of a destabilizing, antiparliamentary right.

At the same time, however, in another characteristic irony of Chilean political development, the very oligarchic unity which allowed stable parliamentary institutions also encouraged unusually strong class cleavages expressed in part through organized partisan conflict. The interpenetration of landed, mining, and commercial wealth made it impossible for any of the parliamentary-based parties to appeal seriously to the class interests of the rural poor or to the increasingly radicalized workers in the new nitrate fields. Political organization of the workers, therefore, was left largely to an "externally-created" and initially revolutionary Marxist movement, led by the Communist and Socialist parties. Mobilization of the peasantry was effectively prevented until the 1950s by repression, suffrage restrictions, and later, by the partial co-optation of Marxist leaders themselves (see Pike, 1963; Angell, 1972, 1966).

For somewhat different reasons, the upper-class parliamentary elite also failed initially to provide access to the amorphous "middle sectors" which began to appear on the scene in the early 1900s. Eventually, as noted, the Radical party did reach out to integrate these sectors into the system. During the parliamentary period, however, the nitrate bonanza prompted most upper-class parliamentarians to remain firmly committed to free trade abroad and to laissez-faire at home; whereas the middle classes, unable to find a secure economic base in the private sector, required an extension of governmental welfare services and the expansion of a patronage bureaucracy. It is important to bear in mind, in short, that even as parliamentary politics took root in the early twentieth century, it did so in an increasingly divided, fissiparous society. This contradiction has in many respects persisted throughout the twentieth century, and it sets the stage, as it were, for our discussion of the pre-authoritarian regime itself.

The economic basis for the pre-authoritarian regime was laid by the third historical-environmental factor presented in the framework—delayed industrialization, spurred in the Chilean case by the collapse of the nitrate market and by the import-substitution incentives provided by international depression and war.

As in many other countries, Chile's immediate response to these pressures was the collapse, rather than the expansion, of the older constitutional order. During the 1920s, the military strongman Carlos Ibáñez was perhaps the most important figure in Chilean politics. Largely as a result of his pressure, a variety of constitutional and legal reforms restructured the Chilean polity in ways designed to cope with the exigencies of industrialization: the powers of the Chilean executive were again strengthened vis-à-vis congress; the economic functions of the state as a whole were expanded; a social security system was instituted; and a labor code, designed simultaneously to structure and control the labor movement, was passed (Nunn, 1970).

Although authoritarian means were initially used to launch these reforms, they were soon taken over by party organizations formed during the earlier period and encompassed within the framework of an expanded constitutional order. The import-substitution processes made possible by these reforms seemed initially to offer something to all of the forces then operating in the Chilean political arena. For the middle class (now led by the Radicals) and the urban and mining workers linked to the Marxist parties, the industrialization process held out the hope of expanded welfare and employment in both the public and private industrial sector. At the same time, with their customary supply of consumer goods cut off by the war and depression, import-substitution no longer appeared particularly threatening to the Chilean right, especially after it realized that this process would not jeopardize the traditional agrarian bases of the right's power and that it could profit considerably from participation within a state-subsidized process of industrialization.

The turning point in the political and economic accommodation between these forces was the election of 1939 in which a center-left alliance of Radicals, Communists, and Socialists captured the Chilean presidency. Economically, this "Popular Front" administration and several center-left successors made explicit the import-substitution policies already tacitly adopted by earlier administrations; it expanded the state planning mechanisms; and it extended further welfare benefits to white and blue-collar supporters of the Radicals and the left. Politically, the victorious Radical-led coalitions of the forties helped to co-opt, at least partially, the main Communist and Socialist leaders into the system. Allende himself, for example, was a cabinet minister during that early period, and served more or less continuously as a senator thereafter. At the same time, the center-left coalition (led after all by the "safe" and "traditional" Radicals) also reassured the right in various ways. Existing elites were assured: that they would have ample access to state credits and subsidies; that the old hacienda system would not be touched; that the rights of foreign and domestic property would be respected; and that the urban-based leftist parties would refrain from attempts to mobilize the rural masses.

These "settlements," made on terms that were highly favorable to established social sectors, were obviously insufficient to put an end to the centrifugal pressures of Chilean society. On the contrary, as the social and economic limitations of import-substitution policies became increasingly clear, political tensions increased substantially, culminating ultimately in the events of September 1973. In the decades after 1939, however, these tensions were channeled to a substantial degree through an increasingly institutionalized party system which seemed over time to become ever more competitive and progressively less bound by the compromises that had initially protected the social and economic power of the Chilean upper and middle classes.

Five major parties comprised the basis of the system. The center, until the 1960s, was dominated by the Radicals, who drew about 20 percent of the congressional vote. Afterward, the more reform-oriented Christian Democrats, who gained support from virtually every stratum of Chilean society, displaced the Radicals as the largest single party. Their share of the electorate peaked at about 40 percent in 1965 and tapered off to 25-30 percent thereafter. The Socialists and Communists, although never fully accepted as legitimate power contenders, were nevertheless permitted a comparatively wide competitive latitude. Their leaders were accepted in legislative and electoral alliances, filled cabinet posts, occupied prominent positions in the congress, sat on municipal councils, secured important positions within the universities, and dominated much of the national union movement. Over the 30 year period, their combined electoral support—spreading from the proletariat to the urban and rural poor—grew from about 20 to 40 percent. On the right, finally, the National party (formed in 1967 by the merger of the Liberals and Conservatives) retained considerable electoral strength. Although their share of the vote declined from about 40 to about 20 percent in the mid-1960s, they continued to marshal support both in rural areas and within the urban middle classes, providing Chile's economic elites with substantial leverage within the constitutional arena. Collectively, these parties, as Valenzuela (1973: 18) argues, became the

> crucial linkage structures binding organizations and institutions at all levels to the political center. Local units of all parties were active within each level of the bureaucracy, each labor union, each student federation, and each professional association, attempting to place its own members in leadership positions. . . . The strategies of the different groups that formed the basis of the Chilean institutional arena were closely interwoven with the activities of the national parties and followed closely the general political life of the nation.

The "political classes" at the apex of these parties, highly skilled and professionalized politicians, did a great deal to hold the system together. Rooted in a legislature which continued to retain considerable strength, leaders drawn from across the party spectrum developed strong self-interest (if not a genuinely internalized commitment) in preserving the constitutional bases of their influence. In spite of the antagonisms of the social sectors they represented, therefore, they were until the very end predisposed to compromise and anxious to avoid the legislative stalemate and political escalation that might bring the system down.

Over time, finally, as the constitutional system began to acquire a "life of its own," it became increasingly open and competitive. Strict limitations on the suffrage, one of the main features of the "settlements" of the 1940s, were the first to disappear. By the late 1960s, the size of the Chilean electorate had tripled, as women, peasants, and the urban poor were mobilized into politics by the left and the Christian Democrats. Concommitantly, as these two political sectors gained in strength, previously "taboo" issues and programs—land reform, control of foreign interests, rural unionization—began to dominate the debate among the parties, replacing the earlier "consensus" on the viability of import-substitution. Eventually, as we now know, the conflict over such questions could not be contained within constitutional bounds. Yet it is a mark of the institutionalization of the system that in 1964 and 1970, successive Christian Democratic and leftist administrations were actually allowed to take office and to seriously implement many of the major structural reforms they had proposed in the electoral arena—a phenomenon that would have appeared inconceivable 30 years earlier.

Historical-Environmental Factors and the Authoritarian-Corporate Infrastructure

The basic weaknesses of Chile's multiparty system have already been implied in the discussion of its evolution: in the classic fashion of the Marxian dialectic, the very features of socioeconomic change which were essential to the development of the Chilean polity served eventually to undermine it. The pattern of Chile's initial integration into the world economy, while allowing for the emergence of a stable parliamentary order, also stimulated the formation of a highly stratified hacienda economy—one which established the basic pattern of class relations for centuries to come and inhibited industrialization until the first quarter of the twentieth century. The import-substitution processes described above, while allowing for some accommodation of white and blue-collar interests, did not eliminate Chilean social inequalities or dependency, and left Chile an economically troubled society. In the 1960s, 14 percent of Chile's population received 42 percent of the national income, while the bottom 60 percent earned only 28 percent. The Chilean economy, still closely tied to the fluctuations of world copper prices, went through several "boom" and "bust" cycles. Overall, however, the rate of growth was low, averaging only 1.6 percent per capita from 1960 to 1970, while prices rose at an annual rate of almost 40 percent during the same period.[5] Throughout the pre-authoritarian period, therefore, a general if diffuse dissatisfaction pervaded virtually all segments of Chilean society—from the newly mobilized urban and rural poor, to the partially-accommodated white and blue-collar sectors (whose gains were constantly eroded by inflation), to the increasingly anxious and insecure economic elites.

Nothwithstanding the emphasis just given to the atypical features of the Chilean party system, these deep social cleavages could never be fully expressed through legislative-electoral channels. In fact, as already implied, a variety of constraints were imposed on Chile's evolution toward pluralism, intertwined within the structure of the constitutional order itself. Although some of these constraints have already been mentioned, they are worth underlining here. For although they were less pronounced than elsewhere, they paralleled at least some of the typical features of an "authoritarian-corporate infrastructure."

In the first place, the growing governmental bureaucracy, rationalized by the state's responsibility for the direction of the economy, remained alongside the legislature as a principal arena for the working out of relations between the new middle sector, the upper class, and the state. For white-collar workers and professionsals, proliferating state agencies, planning boards, ministries, and semi-public bodies provided employment, services, and some security in a situation of job scarcity and price instability. Indeed, in addition to its "manifest" electoral and legislative functions, the most important "latent" function of the Radical party machine had been to offer avenues of access into the state bureaucracy, providing patronage favors and mobility opportunities for its largely middle class clientele.[6]

For the upper class, "corporatist" penetration into the bureaucratic arena served as an important hedge against the vicissitudes of electoral politics. The strength of the rightist parties in congress, in other words, was backed up by the direct representation of the major, elite-dominated peak associations within all important state decision-making bodies. Until at least the mid-1960s, these corporatist arrangements afforded upper class interests with highly significant "nonparty" and "nonlegislative" means of influencing political decision-making. Major peak associations, for example, could often name cabinet-level appointees in ministries relevant to their economic sector. They could veto government initiatives deemed especially harmful to their interests. And they were even able, according to Menges (1966), to regulate new investment in the economic sectors under thier control.

As a result of these "latent" co-optive and corporatist functions, the Chilean public bureaucracy thus became an important bulwark of the established order. Important economic decisions were "parcelled out" to bureaucratic agencies with conservative clienteles. The movement of professionals and white-collar workers into an expanding civil service helped to integrate these sectors into the existing system and tended to produce generally conservative policy orientations among government workers. The haphazard pattern through which this co-optation had occurred—through the ad hoc establishment of new bureaus and semiautonomous agencies—rendered the bureaucracy as a whole structurally resistant to central control and ineffective as an instrument for the implementation of major new policy initiatives (Petras, 1969).

Second, although the Chilean working class did eventually become unusually strong and independent, a variety of economic and legal constraints interfered with this process throughout the pre-authoritarian period. The delayed and dependent character of Chilean economic change was probably the major obstacle to working class organization. Only limited opportunity for industrial employment was afforded by the new manufacturing sector, dominated by small consumer goods firms and by large, high-technology, capital-intensive plants; and the economic strength of the unions which did form in this sector was eroded by the presence of large pools of underemployed workers in the urban service sector and in the countryside.

In addition, the labor code passed in 1925 was designed in many respects to further weaken the union movement. Rural unions, as noted, were in effect outlawed altogether by the labor code, while urban unions were subjected to the possibility of extensive state supervision and important restrictions. In provisions similar to "corporatist" patterns elsewhere, the Chilean labor law required "legal recognition" for new unions, mandated state supervision of union constitutions and leadership selection, established extensive arbitration procedures, and gave the state almost complete control over the investment and use of union funds. In all but a few industrial sectors, moreover, the law confined collective bargaining to the level of the plant, forbidding the formation of effective industry-wide federations and encouraging the fragmentation of the union movement as a whole (Angell, 1972).

To an extent these weaknesses were offset by the organizational activities of the Chilean parties. Since 1940, the Communists and Socialists, and to a lesser extent, the Radicals and Christian Democrats, had successfully championed the bread-and-butter interests of at least some blue-collar sectors, particularly in mining, construction, transportation, and so forth. And in more recent decades, partisan mobilization had penetrated virtually all portions of the lower class. Yet the capacity of this heterogeneous mass to assert its interests stemmed as much from the competitive dynamics of the multiparty system as from industrialization or legal toleration of free association per se. And it is important to remember that these mobiliza-tional efforts occurred in contest of economic scarcity and hierarchical controls, which served to limit the "real" benefits flowing to workers and to increase their alienation.

Given the degree of fragmentation in Chilean society, finally, it should not be surprising that Chileans of all social classes were intermittently at-tracted to a third feature of authoritarian-corporate rule—the idea of a strong, autocratic "center" of authority which might rise above and inte-grate a divided polity. Intermixed with the much noted "pride in Chilean democracy," allegedly a feature of the Chilean political culture, there had always existed a diffuse frustration with the incrementalist style of the parties that dominated the legislature and a general feeling that in such a system "nobody really rules" (Ayres, 1973). Attempts to "transcend" this situation, conversely, constitute recurrent themes in Chilean history, evident in the autocratic republic of Portales, in the popularity of Ibáñez strongman rule in the 1920s, and in the 1925 constitution: re orms which granted enormous legal powers to Chilean presidents (Moreno, 1969).

In the pre-authoritarian period, these tendencies showed through pri-marily in the arena of presidential politics, where several victorious candi-dates attempted to disassociate themselves fully or partially from partisan backing. The former strongman, Ibáñez, was elected in 1952 on an explic-itly antiparty platform; and in 1958, the victor was Jorge Alessandri who, though supported principally by the rightist parties, portrayed himself as a political "independent." Even Eduardo Frei and Allende (the victors in 1964 and 1970 and "party men" to the core) occasionally appealed over the heads of their party organizations in the legislature to "the people" at large.

In an important contrast with other pre-authoritarian regimes, the Chilean military had not since the 1930s been an overt candidate for this sort of "moderating" role. Nevertheless, there is evidence that many Chileans were, in their search for a stabilizing political center, at least receptive to such a possibility. Hansen's (1967) survey of Santiago resi-dents indicate that large majorities of all social classes viewed military officers as less "ambitious" and "corruptible" than politicians, and more "honorable" and "trustworthy"—traits which presumptively qualified officers as potential referees in the political game. Although Hansen's sample opposed long-term military dictatorship, a large majority viewed the armed forces as an appropriate "guardian of the constitutional order," legitimately able to take over government to prevent "anarchy or rebel-lion" and "to end civilian dictatorships." Significantly, military officers shared these civilian orientations. Thus, 86 percent of Hansen's sample of officers (as opposed to 71 percent of civilian middle and upper class respondents) accepted the "constitutional guardianship" function as a proper one for the military establishment—a role conception quite similar to the ones which had conventionally defined civil-military relationships in countries such as Brazil and Peru (Hansen, 1967: 121, 155, 254; Stepan, 1971).

In 1972-1973, on the eve of his overthrow, Allende himself made many of these assumptions explicit. In an effort to stabilize his beseiged administration, he brought military officers into key cabinet and administrative posts for the first time in 30 years. Although the military lacked the "political preparedness" of its counterparts in other countries, this move did (in hindsight, at least) smooth the way for the armed forces' eventual decision to assume direct governmental control (North, 1976).

In the first part of this paper, I argued that in typical cases the "authoritarian-corporate infrastructure" provided an important ground of continuity between the old order and the new one. In Chile, the impact of this infrastructure was diluted and deflected by the institutionalization of the party system described here. Nevertheless, it is important to bear in mind that in some respects the "building blocks" for a new order are present in Chile. Indeed, from a very broad historical perspective, the story of the development of an increasingly competitive party system and its collapse could easily be retold in terms of a gradual deterioration of some aspects of the authoritarian-corporate infrastructure and of a contemporary attempt at their "restoration." The evolution toward pluralism which led to Allende's election had also eroded the right's extralegislative veto power and its bureaucratic controls over labor, allowing fuller political expression of the antagonisms which lay embedded in Chilean society. From this point of view, the reappearance of the military on the scene during the 1970s—its role in the Allende administration as well as its eventual takeover of government—can be understood less as an aberration than as an attempt to restore and rebuild some of the legal and bureaucratic apparatus that for decades had helped to maintain the Chilean social equilibrium.

But all of the other successful transitions occurred in settings where the authoritarian-corporate infrastructure had not been so extensively attenuated—where constitutional structures had broken down rather quickly in the face of political mobilization and economic change. The leaders of Portugal, Spain, Italy, Brazil and Peru could consolidate their new orders preemptively—with a less broadly organized opposition and with a still predominately agrarian economy.[7] The fact that Chile's more institutionalized multiparty system was able to adapt to similar environmental pressures for so long a time has deprived her new rulers of comparable advantages. By the time the system broke down in the 1970s, Chile's authoritarian elite confronted a much more widely politicized population, far more difficult to control through corporatist means; and it faced a more complex "economic problem space," in which easy import-substitution solutions to economic growth requirements had already been exhausted. Perhaps, in other words, the process of political mobilization and economic change has gone "too far" in Chile to make an overt author-itarian-corporatist political formula viable. This possibility, and the dilem-ma it poses, is further explored in the subsequent sections.

THE PRE-AUTHORITARIAN REGIME:
THE MARXISTS AND THE MILITARY

The preceding discussion of the broad outlines of Chilean development affords a clearer perspective for a closer look at some of the atypical fea-tures of the pre-authoritarian regime and its contradictions. The most important general contrast between Chile and other pre-authoritarian re-gimes was that much broader segments of the "real" country were progres-sively mobilized into the "official" constitutional order. As already sug-gested, this difference tended to make the contradictions in the Chilean case more profound than elsewhere. For although party organization of competing interests prolonged the life of the constitutional system and deterred military "praetorianism," it also helped to deepen the polarization of society.

Allende's victory in 1970 brought this contradiction to a head. His narrow electoral plurality was made possible in the first place because the rightist and centrist parties, embittered over the reforms of the previous Christian Democratic administration, could not agree on a common candi-date as they had done in 1964. Once in power, however, Allende's popular unity coalition found itself confronted by an increasingly hostile legis-lature, dominated by opposition parties. To be sure, even at this point the system was by no means completely stalemated. Through the occasional support of the opposition parties or by the use of presidential decree powers, the Allende government began a process of major social trans-formation—eliminating the largest Chilean haciendas, expropriating virtual-ly all foreign enterprises, assuming control of many domestic firms, and accelerating still further the organization of the lower class (see Johnson, 1973: Medhurst, 1972; NACLA, 1972). Yet the radicalization of Chilean politics (all made possible by the institutionalization of the constitutional system itself) carried with it an inevitably destabilizing reaction: increased foreign pressures, land and factory seizures organized by new revolution-ary organizations, armed resistance by ultra-rightist groups, and severe economic deterioration.[8] At the center of this storm were the parties themselves—on the one hand, a well-organized Marxist minority; on the other, Christian Democratic and National politicians who by 1973 were calling publicly from their centers of strength within the congress for the dismantling of the Allende regime.

When it finally came, in short, Chile's version of the "hegemonic crisis" involved a stalemate between entrenched political forces rather than inchoate social movements and tendencies. It is surely this fact above all which explains the extraordinary violence with which the military jerked Chile back toward an authoritarian-corporate "mean." To survive, the military could not simply put Allende on an airplane to Cuba. It had to dismantle the entire institutional apparatus that had allowed him to come to power in the first place—a political exigency that is conveniently ignored by those who welcomed the coup but condemned its "excesses."

The "delayed" impact of this crisis, however, after so many years of civilian mobilization, produced a number of atypical pre-authoritarian features which may now present serious obstacles to a successful completion of this transition. These include:

(1) A competitive relationship between well organized parties of the center and right—in particular the Christian Democrats and the National Party.

(2) A highly mobilized "popular sector" led by Marxist parties.

(3) The political inexperience of the Chilean military, caused by its 30-year retreat from the direct participation in the political arena.

The first of these institutional legacies of the pre-authoritarian period— the organization and competition between representatives of "established" social forces—may well have been altered by the trauma of the past few years, and I shall reserve discussion of it until the treatment of the triggering crisis in the next section. This section gives closer scrutiny to the character of Chile's military rulers and of its principal Marxist and labor opposition. How great is the latter's relative capacity to resist incorporation? What are the inherited debilities of the Chilean military, and to what extent can they be overcome?

Marxist Opposition and Lower Class Organization: The Problems of Incorporation

The ability of a Marxist-led working class to form an effective opposition to the current military government must be evaluated largely in terms of their earlier capacity to overcome the economic and legal constraints on lower class organization mentioned above. The latter, coupled with divisions among Communists and Socialists, and co-optation of Marxist leaders, all converged for several decades to inhibit the massive organization of low status groups. Nevertheless, due to the relative openness of the Chilean constitutional system, the Marxist politicians had long been able to organize relatively broad *electoral* support; and by the 1960s, the competitive race between the Marxists and Christian Democrats had produced an unparalleled growth of lower class *organizations*.

Robert Ayers (1973: 503-504) provides some impressive data in this regard. Between 1964 and 1970, membership in industrial unions increased by almost one-third, from 142,958 to 203,212. More dramatic still was the opening up of the countryside to union penetration. Even before Allende's election, rural union membership had grown from practically zero to 127,688. Altogether, by 1970, an estimated 30 percent of economically active Chileans had been unionized (largely, though not exclusively, by Communists, Socialists, and Christian Democrats). This percentage, while still below Argentina's 34 percent, was almost three times that of Brazil's 11 percent and substantially higher than the percentages registered in most other Latin American countries. None of these figures, finally, takes into account the nonunion lower class organizations which mushroomed in Chile during the 1960s. Ayres estimates that some 66,316 slum dwellers had been organized into assorted community action programs, neighborhood associations, and mothers' centers by 1970; that approximately 100,000 peasant smallholders had been organized into cooperatives and committees; and that about 30,000 rural families had been placed on *asentamientos*.

What does this past history of political mobilization tell us about the current capacity of the Chilean lower classes and their political leaders to resist incorporation? In fact, a good deal of caution must be exercised in drawing conclusions. For one thing, the coup itself shattered the formal apparatus of the Marxist movement. Communist and Socialist Parties, the M.I.R. and the Marxist-dominated labor confederation (the CUT) were outlawed. Tens of thousands of Marxist politicians, union leaders, activists, and ordinary members were killed, jailed, fired, in hiding, or in exile. Changes in the "rules of the game" since 1973, with the new preponderance of coercion as the main political currency, has thus significantly reduced the ability of Marxist leaders to mobilize an effective opposition.

Moreover, if we look behind the figures cited above, it becomes clear that this ability was never as great as it might have appeared on the surface. The Marxist parties, themselves still divided by internal rivalries, had never controlled more than about one-half of the workers' movement, and at times incurred a good deal of antipathy among some lower class elements. Many of the better-paid copper workers, for example, although traditionally Marxist-oriented, had in 1970 voted for the Christian Democrats or the right, apparently out of fear that nationalization of the copper mines would jeopardize their position. Among the poorest workers, many peasant smallholders and hacienda workers, fearful of collectivization, also identified with the Christian Democrats and even with the right (Petras, 1973). The military's decision to parcel out "reformed" agrarian settlements to individual proprietors represents at least one attempt to play upon this fear. Further, even in the workers' sectors "controlled" by the Marxists, the structure of the union movement (oriented toward plant unions rather than larger federations) and the "economistic" orientations of many of the more established labor syndicates placed long-standing limitations on the ability to mobilize workers around political, rather than wage and salary, issues (Angell, 1972; Landsberger, 1967).

These considerations suggest that the potential for the successful lower class demobilization, if not incorporation, does exist in Chile. Her military rulers, it is true, can probably never hope to gain the positive political allegiance of the majority of Chile's workers and peasants. However, if they can successfully control the economic crisis, increase employment opportunities, and retain the support of "established" social and political forces, they may well be able to induce grudging compliance from some workers and to coerce others into sullen apathy and withdrawal, rather than overt opposition.

But, by comparative standards, the *probabilities* of such an outcome in Chile appear considerably lower than those of the other cases. In the Mediterranean countries, Brazil, and Peru, the overall level of political mobilization was low, at least until the very onset of the "triggering crisis." And even then, the mobilizing agents themselves were poorly organized, and the scope of their efforts was restricted to the urban areas or to particular regions. In Spain, for example, where Franco's army faced probably the most extensively mobilized resistence of all the successful cases, the new Spanish rulers could nonetheless count on a degree of support from a traditionalist or parochial peasantry, still alrgely under the sway of the conservative Catholic Church and the rural elites. Extensive political mobilization was also still relatively new in 1964 Brazil, where as in Chile, authoritarian rulers had to depose a labor-oriented government. Thus, these rulers could easily dismantle the still fluid peasant leagues and could reestablish control over an urban working class that had long been accustomed to the control of state-sponsored syndicates. In most of the other cases, the authoritarian-corporatist coup was even more of a preemptive action, taken at a still earlier stage in the upswing of working class consciousness and organization.

In Chile, political mobilization occurred through the dynamics of the political system itself and could be more easily and more routinely assimilated into the framework of the system, reaching a very high level even before the crisis triggered by Allende's election. During Allende's term, moreover, the scope and depth of the mobilization process was extended even further. The government organized workers' participation committees in the nationalized industrial sectors, expanded neighborhood organization, and vastly accelerated the pace of land reform. On the fringes of the constitutional system, the M.I.R. added to his process by organizing seizure of agricultural land, factories, and urban housing sites. Thus, by the end of Allende's administration, the scope of mobilization, building on an already high base of lower class politicization, had extended to virtually every corner of Chilean society.

There is no direct way, of course, to assess the degree of Chilean political *consciousness,* relative to other cases cited. It is clear however, that the spread of lower class political structures was rooted in substantial pociets of pro-Marxist ideological militancy. Prothro and Chaparro's (1974) survey of Santiago residents in 1970 shows that 57 percent of the voters regularly identified with the Marxist parties gave "ideological" reasons (such as, for the workers or against capitalism) to explain their support for Allende.[9] In-depth interviews conducted by Petras (1973) suggest even higher levels of political awareness and collective consciousness among newly organized Mirista and Socialist peasants and pobladores than among the more "economistic" members of the established Marxist trade unions. And although the latter are not easily mobilized over ideological issues per se, they nonetheless have been quite militant in defense of their immediate interests, which are more than likely to be threatened by the current military regime. In short, notwithstanding the unevenness of "class conciousness" in Chile, it is probably fair to say that Chilean workers are more collectively oriented, more aggressive in defense of their interests, more inclined to view the world in terms of class antagonisms than were those in most other Mediterranean and Latin countries.

Given the extensive organizational and psychological roots of the Marxist opposition, Chile's rulers are thus clearly faced with a far more serious demobilization challenge than were those of Brazil and Spain. Structures such as the ones described are far more likely to be driven underground than destroyed completely, and only then with very high levels of coercion, systematically and continuously applied.[10]

Although the picture inside Chile is still unclear as of mid-1975, the government does appear temporarily to have succeeded in its efforts at demobilization. The Socialists, who were always relatively disorganized and who bore the main brunt of the 1973 resistance, are in serious disarray. And, as noted, the leaders of the MIR and of the Communist Party have been quite systematically hunted down or driven into exile. On the other hand, it is probable that a good deal of the infrastructure of these groups—especially of the Communist Party—remains intact, with lower and middle level cadres organized in cellular fashion and difficult to root out. This network of continuing loyalties and communications provides a potential for strong pressures on the regime and a continuing threat to its long-term stabilization.

The conversion of this general threat into more concrete forms of opposition is likely to be contingent on the relative unity of the dominant sectors of the new regime. United, Chile's rulers are unlikely to be toppled by lower-class resistance. But even small cracks in the structure of power may release, and then be widened by, strong pressures from below. Acts of terrorism, sabotage, kidnapping, and the like could well follow any serious effort to relax the strict surveillance and control which now prevail in Chile. And if Chilean rulers divide seriously among themselves and/or lose the support of established civilian sectors, the political costs of repression may be too high to prevent more massive forms of working-class protest, such as the strikes and demonstrations which produced the collapse of the Ongania regime in Argentina.

In the light of the above, it is not surprising that, after almost two years in power, the Chilean junta had not yet attempted to replace existing lower class organizations with an alternative, corporatist syndical structure (Latin America, 1974c: 86). Indeed, it is difficult to conceive how such a structure could ever amount to more than a paper organization. To make it more than this would require not only the wholesale purging of existing political and union leaders (a task, ironically, which in some ways is made more difficult by the highly decentralized, plant-based structure of the Chilean union movement), but also the recruitment of an entirely new politically-neutral union cadre which can maintain at least some contact with a highly politicized worker and peasant population. The establishment of new corporatist structures would also require almost continual monitoring and supervision to insure that (as in Argentina) militant opposition elements did not infiltrate back into positions of leadership. Finally, if Brazil is a model, it would require a control structure with enough "slack" so that some benefits could be provided and some grievances aired, without at the same time having such processes unleash the submerged antagonisms and partisan loyalties developed in the pre-authoritarian regime (see Schmitter, 1971).

The Governing Capacity of the Chilean Armed Forces

A significant reciprocate of the development of Chile's post-1940 multi-party system was the retreat of the military from active involvement in the day-to-day politics of that country. In the prior period, to be sure, the army, led by Carlos Ibáñez, had played a significant role in mediating the integration of the "middle sectors" into the system. Even afterwards, cliques of officers continued intermittently to engage in political action, although with declining frequency. And, as we have seen, the *attitudes* of both civilian society and the military establishment were in some ways supportive of a more active "guardianship" role. But from the mid-1930s until at least the end of the 1960s, as the conflicts of Chilean society came more and more to be funneled through the party structure, such attitudes ceased to be transformed directly into overt political behavior.[11] Thus, at the same time that the institutionalization of the Chilean system was creating the basis for a highly mobilized opposition to military rule, it was also stimulating the recruitment of several generations of relatively po- litically-inexperienced military officers who now must form the center of the new political order. Let me look more closely at this problem in a comparative context.

The military establishments of "typical" pre-authoritarian regimes were politically active on a much more continuous and direct basis, even when they did not actually take over the reins of government. They constituted, in the first place, arenas within which contending civil-military factions vied for power. And, even more important, the armed forces as institu- tional units frequently acted as referees in the struggles occurring else- where in the system. These roles it should be noted, were not necessarily inconsistent with the "professionalization" of the armed forces (unless this term is defined tautologically to mean political noninvolvement). Especially in Brazil and Peru—where the most recent of the authoritarian- corporate coups have occurred—relatively integrated national infrastruc- tures (and U.S. training programs?) laid the basis for the development of highly institutionalized military establishments, with at least some corpo- rate insulation from the policy disputes taking place among civilians. In these cases particularly, the combination of political participation and pro- fessionalization seem, in at least two ways, to have contributed signifi- cantly to the emergence of military-dominated authoritarian-corporatist regimes.

First, in both countries professional military roles came to be defined at least partly in terms of acquiring the expertise perceived as necessary for developing and managing a complex industrial society. This was re- flected in both countries by, among other things, the establishment of advanced war academies which in the 1950s were offering courses in such topics as economics, planning, and sociology. And by the time the mili- taries assumed permanent governmental authority in the 1960s, this meant that they could draw on a fairly wide reservoir of officers-cum-technocrats with a good deal of training, practical experience, self-confidence, and a sense of their own political superiority vis-à-vis civilians (see Stepan, 1971; Einaudi, 1973; Payne, 1968).

Second (this is a proposition which requires much additional research), I would argue that by the time they took over in the mid-1960s, the Peruvian and Brazilian militaries had evolved a variety of rather unusual "consultative techniques" for sounding out opinions and deliberating policy, which may have helped them to sustain their institutional cohesion while in office.

In most military establishments (Brazil's and Peru's included), formal command structures and/or informal, often secret cliques and followings form the main apparatus of decision-making. But these, by themsleves, are not very efficient means of maintaining the level of internal communication and bargaining necessary for sustained military control of the state. In Brazil and Peru, however, a variety of more systematic and more flexible arrangements have tended to supplement such processes. In both countries, for example, the national war colleges were not only training institutes, but forums of discussion in which the militaries' "national development" missions were debated and hammered out. In Brazil, periodic elections within the Military Club were regularly considered devices for sounding out policy positions within the officer corps. And in Peru, before the 1962 coup d'etat, the officers' political preferences were actually polled by Peruvian military commanders (Stepah, 1971; Payne, 1968; Skidmore, 1967). These and other devices (see expecially Lowenthal's [1974] discussion of the Peruvian C.O.A.P.) may partially explain why both military establishments have adapted surprisingly well to the day-to-day exigencies of governance. The Brazilians, after all, have managed peacefully to select four successive chief executives, in spite of their internal divisions; and the Peruvians have since 1968 gone through a variety of major policy changes without major disruption.

How does the Chilean military stack up against these "models" of "governing capacity?" In at least two respects, it does fairly well. First, by most indications, the Chileans had acquired a rather high degree of institutional autonomy and corporate cohesion—the result, among other things, of their lack of political involvement. According to Hansen (1967: 169), professional standards had long governed both the recruitment and promotion of officers. Entry into the officer corp require graduation from an *Escuela Militare*, the U.S. equivalent of three years of high school and the first two years of college; increasingly, promotion came to depend on additional academic training and achievement, either in the War Academy or the Polytechnical Institute. Hansen's study also suggests that, while there was considerable contact between officers and civilians, an army career to a large extent involved officers in a relatively self-contained world. Thus, 26 percent of Hansen's officer sample (as opposed to only 11 percent in the United States) were recruited directly from military families. Four-fifths of the "best friends" listed by respondents were themselves military officers. Although about half of Hansen's sample did belong to civilian clubs such as the Rotary or sports clubs, all were also members of military associations and 37 percent belonged solely to such groups. It should be added, finally, that since the 1930s the legal prohibitions and informal norms against "political" activities of any sort had been strictly upheld. Few retired officers and no active ones belonged to parties, ran for elective office, or held high governmental positions (1967: 172-178).

Second, notwithstanding some indications of serious cleavages within the Chilean armed forces, the degree of pre-coup political dissension was probably no more profound—and possibly even less so—than among Brazilian and Peruvian officers. Here, however, we enter onto highly speculative ground. The Chilean navy and air force were reputedly always more conservative than the army—an impression which is consistent with the alleged "moderation" of General Pinochet, relative to his other colleagues on the current junta. "Constitutionalist" majorities in all branches, moreover, were probably initially quite reluctant to follow the lead of their more militant colleagues in the overthrow of Allende. And still more serious divisions are suggested by the reports of confrontations with pro-Allende garrisons in September and by the subsequent military trials of considerable numbers of high-ranking officers (Latin America, 1973c).

On the other hand, the strong norms of partisan neutrality probably helped to insulate the Chilean military even more than their Brazilian and Peruvian counterparts from the left-right divisions of civilian society. Further, the "constitutionalist" scruples of Chilean officers were, by 1973, probably more than counterbalanced by the pervasive civilian and self-definitions of their "guardianship" function. Indeed, given these attitudinal predispositions and the polarized situation of Allende's last year, the coup could be rationalized as an act not only consistent with, but dictated by the military's commitment to sustain the constitution.[12] Viewed in this light, the vigor with which the junta has purged military dissidents is as likely a sign of internal strength as of weakness.

In these respects, then, the Chilean armed forces do not compare unfavorably to the Brazilians and Peruvians at the onset of their political adventures. In fact, this does much to explain why, in all three cases, the takeovers were conducted by the military as corporate institutions, rather than by smaller cliques, civil-military coalitions, or strongmen. When we consider the question of role expansion and consultative apparatus, however, the picture in Chile looks very different.

In contrast to the Peruvians and the Brazilians, technocratic-political orientations had not been widely built into the professional role structure of the Chilean military. Traditionally, Chilean officers had not, like their counterparts, run for elective office, served on boards-of-directors in semi-public corporations, sat on planning boards, or served in ministeries. This picture, to be sure, had been changed substantially by Allende's policy of appointing officers to key administrative posts and to the cabinet itself (see Rojas, 1973; North, 1976). But even assuming that these officers were not purged or rendered politically suspect by their "complicity" with the Allende regime, their three-year experience seems fleeting when compared to more than a decade of similar activities by several generations of Peruvian and Brazilian officers. Prior to Allende, the military's "civic action" responsibilities had been confined, by comparative standards, to a very narrowly defined set of activities: building roads and bridges, conducting literacy programs for conscripts, providing earthquake relief, and acting as backup forces for the police in putting down riots or demonstrations.

This relative inexperience is made more striking still by the fact that, as late as the mid-1960s (a time when the Peruvians and Brazilians had already evolved broad conceptions of their "national development" missions), Chilean officers were still highly divided over even the modest forms of civic action then underway. While 38 percent of Hansen's (1967: 226) sample of active officers preferred an increase in such programs, an equal percentage wanted to *decrease* these activities, arguing that they threatened traditional military roles and diverted available resources from the conventional tasks of national defense.[13] These orientations undoubtedly changed a good deal by September 1973, partially in imitation of the Brazilian and Peruvian examples. It is also clear, however, that the Chileans had not, like the latter, spent the decade hammering out a clear conception of an expanded "developmental mission" which might rationalize or legitimate extended rule. And although the Chilean junta has currently mobilized a host of active and retired officers to oversee a wide range of formerly civilian activities, they cannot draw on a very broad pre-existing reservoir of technocratic talent. Until such talent is recruited and trained, therefore, the Chilean military center may be comparatively dependent on the support and compliance of middle and upper class civilians—on the legitimacy accorded by these elements and their representatives to working for a military-dominated government.

For most of the same reasons, Chilean military institutions also lacked the relatively elaborate consultative apparatus which had been developed by the Peruvians and Brazilians. The former, of course, had had its share of cliques and secret societies, but the restrictions on internal "political" discussions had inhibited any more overt or systematic form of communications and decision-making. Contrast, for example, the above mentioned 1962 poll of Peruvian officers with the internal events leading up to the September coup. In Chile, under the leadership of then-Commander-in-Chief Carlos Prats, the military accepted Allende's bid to reenter his cabinet in the summer of 1973. This had occurred, however, in the face of an apparent mounting political disaffection within the officers' corps as a whole, which ultimately could not be contained through reliance on the "normal" command relationship or on personal loyalties. The first major sign of this dissension came with the abortive tank attack on the Presidential Palace in June 1973. The following August, internal discord was finally resolved not through behind-the-scenes negotiation, but by a noisy demonstration of officers' wives outside of Prat's residence, followed by a hastily-convened conclave of senior officers in Santiago, which forced Prat's resignation and thus cleared the way for the coup.

After the coup, moreover, the Chileans' consultative apparatus remained quite crude by Brazilian and Peruvian standards. The Chilean junta, led by Pinochet, remained the principal decision-making body, apparently responsible for all major foreign policy, economic, and political decisions. This was not, however, underpinned by a particularly elaborate network of military coordinating committees, civil-military advisory bodies, or political supervisory and control structures. Leaders of the major civilian *gremios* and peak associations who supported the coup, instead consulted on a relatively ad hoc basis with members of the junta themselves or with other key officers. And, until recently, many major political decisions were delegated entirely to practically autonomous provincial military commanders, who exercised their responsibility without extensive guidance or control (Latin America, 1974a).

Of course, these practices may become more systematic as the Chilean military begins to respond to the exigencies of extended political rulership. They have, after all, the advantages of a professionalized and relatively cohesive officers corps, of having purged suspected dissidents, and of being able to learn from the Peruvian and Brazilian examples. But the Chileans begin their task of institution-building from a relatively primitive starting point. If they cannot succeed in overcoming this initial disability, the military *government* is likely to become increasingly remote from the military *establishment*. And as the former grapples with problems—how to deal with civilian sectors, how to cope with foreign policy and domestic economic questions, and how to structure the "new order"—the threat of destabilizing internal coups increases.

THE TRIGGERING CRISIS AND ESTABLISHED GROUPS (1973-1974)

As was true at so many other junctures in Chilean history, the critical "swing" sectors in the attempted transition to authoritarian-corporatist rule are the "established" upper and middle class civilians, their gremial organizations, and their political representatives. Like their counterparts in other successful transitions, these sectors constitute potential "pillars of support" for the new regime—or possibly fatal sources of opposition— a pivotal role which is magnified even more in the Chilean case by the high levels of lower class political mobilization and the initial debilities of the new military rulers. The behavior of these "established" sectors is conditioned by an interaction between two sets of forces: the representational structures inherited from the pre-authoritarian period, and the changes in these patterns produced by the events, choices, and political traumas of the past few "crisis" years (roughly, from the last year or so of the Allende administration to the present).

In the pre-authoritarian regime many "establishment" interests (as well as those of some working class sectors) had been represented by competing "political classes," set apart from many of their constitutents by their interests in preserving the electoral-constitutional bases of their influence, and from one another by their division into well-defined rightist and centrist organizations, with roots in overlapping but distinguishable social sectors (Kaufman, 1972). This, as noted, had been one of the "exceptional" characteristics of the Chilean pre-authoritarian regime, and considered by itself, suggests the possibility of considerable resistance to extended military rule.

The greatest non-Marxist criticism of military rule, as might be expected, has come from sectors oriented toward the centrist Christain Democrats. The moderate reformism and "constitutionalist" orientation of that party's leaders made them more inclined than the right to oppose long-term military rule. Prior to the last year of the Allende administration, many Christian Democratic leaders, despite their "anti-Marxism," had engaged in varying degrees of cooperation with the left. Morevoer, of the various "established" sectors, Christian Democratic followers were most likely to be touched by repression aimed principally at extirpating the Marxist parties. The junta's imprisonment or execution of young middle class radicals (often from "respectable" families); its sometimes indiscriminate efforts to purge the universities of "undesirable" students and professors; the imposition of strict controls over television, radio, and the press; and the stern treatment of all white-collar and lower class unions (many Christian Democratic in orientation)—all affect Christian Democrats as well as Marxists. Predictably, therefore, some Christian Democratic leaders who initially welcomed the coup have subsequently condemned its "excesses." Church officials, long linked informally to the Christian Democratic movement, have also been critical of the junta's policies, and have attempted to shield political fugitives from vengeful military authorities (Latin America, 1974b).

Leaders of the rightist National party have backed the present junta much more enthusiastically. The upper class constituency of this party, after all, has been the principal beneficiary of the coup, and many National politicians themselves have been called upon by the military to fill important advisory roles in the new government. Nevertheless, rightist party leaders, like the Christian Democrats, were members of a political class which had something to lose by long-term military rule. Their party, like the Christian Democrats, has been declared "in recess" by the junta; their press organs have been censored; and changes in the rules of the game have destroyed the accustomed constitutional bases of their influence. It is at least conceivable, therefore, that at some point elements of the political right might also become more critical of the new regime, although their criticism would certainly be less vociferous than that of the Christian Democrats.

Thus, to an extent, both the Christian Democrats and the Nationals constitute potential centers of opposition to the formation of a new, authoritarian-corporatist order. The fact that both sectors had developed fairly sophisticated organizations, and that both have more freedom of movement and more resources than the Marxists, all constrain the Chilean military from following the "Brazilian path" of legally excluding them from the new political system. And the substantial ideological differences between the Christian Democrats and the Nationals make it more difficult for the Chileans to follow the "Spanish path" of allowing co-opted politicos of the Catholic center and right to continue their rivalries within a new authoritarian framework.

But these patterns, largely the spillovers from the earlier, pre-authoritarian era, must be viewed in the context of the incredible trauma of the Allende years and their aftermath. If, by comparative standards, the articulation of centrist and rightist parties was unusual, the characteristics of Chile's "triggering crisis" were even more so. In no other country, after all, had such an explicitly leftist movement come so close to gaining its objectives through participation within a competitive electoral framework. In no other country had established interests been so thoroughly shaken by reforms undertaken within a legal, constitutional order. This new situation—new for Chile as well as for the other countries—constitutes a triggering crisis of much greater proportions than elsewhere and can thus be expected to have a profound impact on the conventional alignments among established political and social sectors. This impact can be examined, as suggested, by considering the cross-pressures generated by the "mobilization" and "economic" issues raised in the current situation.

The Mobilization Aspects of the Chilean Crisis

Even before 1970, of course, broad sectors of Chilean society, mostly from the upper and middle classes, viewed Chile's Marxist movement with considerable distrust. In 1967, for example, over one-half of a sample of Santiago residents (and almost three-quarters of those with any opinion) viewed the Communists and Socialists as "people with dictatorial ideas" (Ayres, 1973: 510). As long as these groups remained a relatively powerless opposition, many people who held such attitudes could adopt a tolerant, live-and-let-live position with regard to Marxist participation n electoral politics.[14] Their actual experience with a "socialist" government, however, seems to have brought their fears to the surface as never before. From the point of view of the established social sectors represented by the right and the Christian Democrats, Allende's nationalization of industrial property, his accelerated land reform program, his tolerance of land and factory seizures, and the increasing organization and militancy of previous apolitical sectors of the lower class, all left little doubt about the "revolutionary" intention of the new regime. Throughout the final year or so Allende's administration, these fears helped to set in motions an escalating process of mobilization and countermobilization, threat and counter-threat, which polarized Chile in unprecedented fashion and generated new incentives for acquiescence to permanent military rule (Fleet, 1973; Angell, 1974; Plastrik, 1974; Sweezy, 1973; Sigmund, 1974).

One consequence, as well as cause, of this polarization process is the deteriorated position of the Christian Democratic (PDC) "center" of the old party system. This deterioration had begun in the late 1960s, as dissension increased between Christian Democratic left and right wings, and as the PDC's electoral support declined. Even after 1970, however, the PDC remained Chile's largest single party and, for a time, a relatively flexible and stabilizing opposition vis-à-vis the Allende administration. Christian Democratic congressional votes had ratified Allende's electoral victory in the first place, facilitating his peaceful accession to the presidency; and Christian Democrats also supported the passage of several governmental initiatives, including the nationalization of the American copper mines. But as both government policies and the opposition to these policies grew more radical in 1972-1973, the Christian Democratic position hardened. By September 1973, Christian Democratic leaders had broken off "dialogue" over Allende's legislative program, openly called for Allende's ouster, and welcomed the coup which came in response to these calls.

For our purposes, it is beside the point whether the hardening Christian Democratic opposition to the Allende government was "provoked" by the left or could have been averted with more flexible centrist leadership. What is important is that, as a result of the events of 1972-1974, the Christian Democrats have been widely and perhaps permanently discredited as a viable centrist governmental alternative, acceptable to both "extremes" and to the military itself. From the viewpoint of many Marxists, the recent Christian Democratic behavior exposed their "true reactionary colors" as staunch defenders of the status quo when the chips are down. On the other hand, rightists and many military leaders attributed the post-1970 Marxist "revolution" at least in part to the Christian Democrats' earlier "reformism," dubbing Eduardo Frei the "Kerensky" to Allende's "Lenin." Finally, in the bloody aftermath of the coup the Christian Democrats themselves seem to have lost the self-confidence and purpose of an earlier time, engaging in bitter internal recriminations over their earlier support of the coup and debating uncertainly over what to do now.

A second important consequence of Chile's mobilization crisis was to alter the customary relationship between Chile's centrist and rightist "political classes" and their upper and middle class constituents. Prior to the 1970s, the politicians, though sharing their representative functions with peak associations and "gremios," had often exerted a restraining influence on the latter's tendency to engage in "direct-action" activities (Kaufman, 1972). But the threat to these interests posed by the Allende government, compounded undoubtedly by mounting hysteria on all sides, often found the "politicos" following rather than leading the anti-Marxist opposition. By 1972-1973, the middle classes, like their counterparts in Goulart's Brazil, had taken their opposition to Allende into the streets; the antiparty Fatherland-and-Liberty movement and relatively extremist "gremios" had become the cutting edges of the efforts to "stop Marxism;" and producers strikes, mass demonstrations, and vigilantism—modes of action often resisted by both rightist politicos and Christian Democrats—became the order of the day. Since the coup. moreover, it is noteworthy that the Chilean junta has turned primarily to the gremial leaders and the heads of the major peak associations, rather than to the rightist party leaders, as the main centers of support (Howe, 1973). Although the relations between military officers, party leaders, and gremialists are still quite fluid, it is doubtful that the electorally-oriented politicos will ever be able to regain the position of predominance they once enjoyed in Child's multi-party system.

Finally, the intensified "revolutionary threat," coup d'etat, and subsequent repression is a process which has burned many important bridges between all segments of the "establishment" and the left itself. The main lesson which many Marxists are bound to draw from this experience is that the "electoral road" to socialism is an illusion to be shunned in favor of more violent, revolutionary forms of political action.[15] For the military, which is likely to be the target of such activities, this threat of reprisals compounds the risks of leaving political office and increases the temptation to add to the vicious circle by engaging in even more repression. Among the broader civilian sectors that had supported the coup, an analogous problem exists: even should they desire reconciliation with the Marxists, they are likely to find the latter less moderate and more anti-system than before.

Thus, the dynamics of the mobilization crisis have tended to push the civilian center, rightist groups, and the military itself into each others' arms. Given the dangers, both real and imagined, now posed by an alienated left, the reintegration of Marxist parties into a restored electoral framework is virtually inconceivable—at least for the intermediate future. An "Argentine" solution, which would restore party politics without Marxists, would, as noted in the introduction, provide a more acceptable alternative to established social and political forces. But civilian governments selected in this fashion would, like the Frondizi and Illia regimes in Argentina, lack both legitimacy and coercive capacity. In addition, they would be continually tempted to "open the Pandora's box" by making deals with the excluded Marxists in order to strengthen their position. It is thus not surprising that, so far, neither Christian Democrats nor rightists seem to find this prospect a very palatable alternative to continued military rule.

The Economic Crisis

Unfortunately for would-be prognosticators, the *economic* aspect of the triggering crisis creates a contradictory set of incentives. Like the mobilization crisis, the exacerbation of Chile's economic difficulties began in the third year or so of Allende's administration and continued throughout the first nine months of military rule. Its features are well known: a sharp decline in agricultural production; chronic shortages of consumer goods normally available to the Chilean middle class; a decline in copper revenues; extreme shortages of foreign exchange reserves (in October 1973 the Central Bank had enough to finance only two days of imports); and most of all, an incredible inflationary spiral that had reached 700 percent by 1974 (Latin America, 1974b). Again, it is not really necessary to decide who was to blame for these conditions. The point is that they constituted a crisis of extreme proportions and may well have been enough to topple the Allende government even if it had not been explicitly "socialist" and redistributive.

But unlike the mobilization threat, the economic collapse not only stimulated the overthrow of the Allende government but threatens its successor as well. Failure to get on top of this crisis is almost certain to drive a wedge between the military and its civilian supporters; and in fact, some signs of disaffection have already occurred over the military government's apparent inability to contain the enormous inflationary pressures. Leaders of the Valparaiso bus drivers' union—one of the major anti-Allende gremios—were arrested after demonstration protesting the rising price of fuel. Middle and upper class housewives, whose anti-Allende protests earlier received much American publicity, have also reportedly registered displeasure over food price increases. And even the editorial pages of the staunchly promilitary *El Mercurio* have admitted, in a guarded criticism of the current government, that "those who thought that military rule would be sufficient to bring spare parts, new investment, and price stability were very far from the truth" (Latin America, 1974b; 1974a).

The military, to be sure, does have some important "advantages" over its Marxist predecessor in dealing with these problems: it is, for one thing, much freer to shift many of the burdens of inflation and shortages back onto the shoulders of the lower classes. A cancellation of the huge minimum wage increases scheduled by the Allende government was one of the first economic decisions made by the new government—presumably to restrict the level of consumer demand and the amount of currency in circulation. In the hope of stimulating increases in the production of consumer goods and their availability to middle class consumers, military leaders also restored nationalized domestic industries to their former managers, dismantled the state-run distribution centers set up in the urban slums, and lifted price controls. Such measures (especially the last) did little in the short-run to contain inflation, and they imposed terrible hardships on the poor, who were now faced with rising prices, frozen wages, *and* scarcities. But they probably helped for the time being to make life somewhat easier for members of the middle class (Latin America, 1973a).

In more general terms, it should be noted that the overall economic policy adopted by the Chilean junta bears a close resemblance to the "recovery" plan that seemed to work so well for the Brazilians in 1964: strict austerity to combat inflationary pressures, devaluations to improve export possibilities, and attempts to attract new foreign capital as an engine to further economic growth. Such measures involve formidable social and political costs; but in the Brazilian case, they did work to bring prices under control and to dramatically expand the gross national product; they offer at least the hope of a similar outcome in Chile (see Graham and McCoy, 1975).

Finally, and most important, the junta does not, like its civilian predecessors, have to answer to an angry electorate. It faces far fewer constraints on the use of coercive apparatus to crush dissent.

But notwithstanding these advantages, the current economic crisis and its attendant political dilemmas will not be easily surmounted in Chile. The dimensions of the crisis, in the first place, are far greater than those faced by the Brazilians in 1964. The Chilean inflation rate alone was ten times that of the Brazilians—a difference which in many respects creates a qualitatively different problem (Graham and McCoy, 1975: 27). Moreover, the results of serious efforts to contain such problems (even if they might prove successful in the long run) are not likely to become visible for a number of years. In the interim, both the economic problems and efforts to deal with them are likely to arouse substantial antagonisms. The devaluations necessary to aid the export sector threaten both domestic producers and consumers. Credit restrictions, salary freezes, tax increases, and other austerity measures are likely, as before, to be bitterly resented by white-collar as well as blue-collar sectors of Chilean society (see O'Donnell, 1973: 115-166). Historically, such measures in Chile have set off a scramble among organized interests to minimize their own share of the burden and to maximize that of others. The severity of the current inflation and the dislocations it has caused seem to require even "harsher medicine" than usual—and therefore considerable unpopularity for the government which attempts to impose this medicine.

It should be remembered finally that the current economic crisis has occurred in the context of an already sluggish, inflationary economy— lacking the "easy" import-substitution possibilities of, say, Mexico in the 1930s, without the export resources or large domestic market of Peru and Brazil, and dominated historically by often inefficient financial and industrial cartels and vested bureaucratic interests. Therefore, even if the Chilean military does manage to contain the immediate economic crisis, it operates within a set of historic parameters that pose serious obstacles to long-term growth. Overcoming these obstacles, assuming that is possible, will almost certainly involve considerable challenge to the vested upper and middle class interests that initially constituted the junta's main civilian source of support. Thus, like virtually all Chilean governments in preceding decades, the junta is damned if it makes "hard" economic decisions—and damned if it does not. And, unlike their counterparts in Brazil, Spain, or Mexico, the Chilean rulers will not soon have the advantage of presiding over an expanding economy in which benefits "trickle down" (however unevenly) to segments of the middle and lower class.

Aspects of the mobilization crisis may, as noted, partially offset these difficulties. Ironically, for example, the nationalization policies and land reform programs of the Allende government have probably increased the military's flexibility vis-à-vis the "dispossessed" segments of Chile's financial, agricultural, and industrial elites. The latter, now dependent on the junta to restore some of their privileges, may be more than previously inclined to accept government-imposed anti-inflation "sacrifices" in exchange for their reintegration into the economic power structure. And the anti-Marxist fears of most "established" middle and upper class groups may make them more tolerant than usual of a governmental failure to deal with inflation and stagnation, especially given the political risks of a return to civilian rule. Yet the threshold of such tolerance is likely to be much lower among the middle than the upper classes. The broad range of white-collar workers, government employees, small bourgeoisie, and professionals—those who in many ways dealt the fatal blow to the Allende government—had fewer privileges to lose in the first place and, consequently, are less dependent on the new military government. They are, in addition, more likely than the upper class to suffer from inflation and more likely still to suffer heavily from anti-inflationary measures. Either way, their economic outlook is bleak and their chances of alienation are high.

Disaffection of the Chilean "middle sectors" will almost certainly carry with it a number of negative political consequences for military rule: greater opposition from centrist politicos, an exacerbation of internal military factionalism, more opportunities for union protest, lower class and white-collar demonstrations, and leftist revolutionary activities. As such tensions increasingly rise to the surface, the political costs of continued repression will also almost certainly continue to mount. And while the current government or some civil-military successor may find it well worthwhile to pay such costs, the trade-offs will become increaingly unclear. Thus, the economic pressures create a structure of incentives which may well prompt the current junta (or some rival civil-military faction) to retreat into the background and let some civilian government take the heat.

THE INTERNATIONAL CONTEXT

In a situation in which the military government is attempting to buy the "political time" in which to put Chile's economic house in order, the supports flowing from the international environment may weigh critically in the balance. On the surface, one might expect this support to be considerable. American government and corporate officials, after all, were strongly opposed to the Allende regime and, as we now know, contributed materially to its collapse. They may well be disposed to accept the present junta as a far more acceptable alternative. Nevertheless, it is one thing to work for the "destabilization" of a "communist" government, and quite another to invest the massive economic resources and diplomatic support necessary to "stabilize" its successor. From this point of view, the prospects of the current junta do not (from its own perspective) appear encouraging.

Let us turn first to the question of economic support. In some respects, the junta is likely to fare considerably better than its immediate predecessor. For example, in early 1974 it managed to renegotiate Chile's enormous foreign debt (estimated at over three billion dollars) with U.S. and European creditor nations, and it has been able to attract some support from lending institutions such as the International Monetary Fund, which recently approved a $79 million line of credit. Moreover, by agreeing to a compensation settlement of more than $350 million with the expropriated American copper companies, the government has won some promises of technological assistance and marketing aid; and it has probably improved overall its prospects of attracting additional foreign investment.

Nevertheless, for several reasons these sources of support—which are central aspects of the junta's overall strategy for economic recovery—are not likely to be sufficient to turn the Chilean situation around. In the first place, in the aftermath of Allende's massive expropriations, Chile will have to pay an exorbitantly high price to lure investment from abroad. The compensation agreement reached with the copper companies, itself a substantial burden on Chile's external financial position, is only one example of the many concessions which the new government seems willing to undertake (Graham and McCoy, 1975: 7). But even with these concessions, foreign investors are not likely to rush into Chile with sizeable sums until it is clear that an economic and political stabilization is in fact underway. This places the junta in something of a squeeze between the need to resolve its political-economic crisis through foreign capital and foreign investors who are likely to wait for the dust to settle before risking their funds.

It should be noted, moreover, that these difficulties come in the context of the highly troubled world economy of the 1970s, rather than the more prosperous economy of the preceding decade. A regime such as Brazil's, established in the 1960s, could count on an expanding demand for its export products and on relatively cheap prices for its vital imports. It could look for investment help not only in the U.S., but also in Europe and Japan, where increasingly favorable trade balances had produced a dramatic accumulation of "Eurodollars." For Chile, the situation is almost exactly the reverse. Demand for its principal export, copper, has dropped substantially. Cost of raw materials, especially petroleum, have skyrocketed. The massive transfer of dollar resources to the oil-producing countries has had a double-barreled effect, diminishing the investment resources of European and American corporate investors and concentrating resources in the hands of OPEC countries which tend to reinvest in the "advanced" countries rather than in the Third World (Graham and McCoy, 1975: 31).

It is reasonably clear, finally, that for the immediate future Chile will not be able to count on anything approaching the level of public aid which helped to prop up the Brazilians in 1964 or, for that matter, the Chilean governments which preceded Allende in the mid-1960s. The Ford administration may be able to push through relatively small amounts of military assistance and emergency loans. But public and congressional support for foreign aid in general has diminished considerably in the past ten years; and the current congress, having already flexed its muscles with respect to Turkey and Indochina, is unlikely to countenance a massive flow of aid dollars to a country with Chile's international reputation. This reluctance parallels that of many European governments which, in 1975, succeeded in postponing a second-round renegotiation of Chile's foreign debt, largely to signify their opposition to the repressive policies of the Chilean junta.

This brings us to the question of international diplomatic and ideological support; and in this area, the junta's prospects appear even bleaker than in the economic sphere. Among the Chilean middle sectors, to be sure, the junta's claim to have saved Chile from "communism" may give it considerable mileage , at least in the short-run. In the 1970s atmosphere of international detente, however, an "anti-communist" appeal is not likely to take the junta as far as it would have in the 1950s and 1960s, even though it may attract at least some covert support in conservative international circles. In this respect, the junta's need to engage in particularly brutal domestic repression (a need which grows out of the extraordinarily mobilized character of Chile's pre-authoritarian regime) works seriously against its international position. For this repressiveness tends to counteract the mobilization of foreign anti-communist sympathies and makes it difficult for all but the most reactionary sectors to lend overt moral support to the junta. We thus encounter another vicious circle, in which the exigencies of anti-communist political consolidation at home diminish the possibilities of attracting diplomatic backing abroad.

Even if diplomatic memories of Chilean repression fade, moreover, there remains for the junta the problem of finding some internationally acceptable "legitimacy formula" that might justify long-term authoritarian-corporate rule. In its search for such a formula, the junta has been influenced by various conservative Chilean intellectuals who, as noted, combine the symbols of Chile's past with some of the language of Mediterranean corporatism. In the postwar world, however, this rhetoric has little international currency. This conservative social doctrine, as Juan Linz noted, has been largely abandoned by international Catholicism itself. "Not only have large sections of Belgian, German, Dutch, and French Catholicism abandoned such ideas, but so have recent popes, whereas in the past many of the popes could be interpreted as preferring if not prescribing such a corporatist approach to politics" (Linz, 1973: 242). In any event, in the aftermath of World War II, corporatist language is far too easily linked to facism.

The absence of a viable legitimacy formula is a problem, of course, not only for Chile, but for all authoritarian-coroporate regimes which have emerged since the 1930s. In the article just cited, Linz notes how difficult it is, even for an apparently stable regime such as Brazil's, to legitimate authoritarian-corporate practices; and he argues that the uneasy juxtaposition of such practices with liberal-democratic rhetoric inhibits the full institutionalization of the Brazilian order. If the problem affects all postwar regimes, however, it is particularly acute in the Chilean case; for Chile, as we have seen, lacks many of the other pre-authoritarian and situational factors which in the Brazilian case helped to offset the absence of international ideological support. In the event of prolonged failure to resolve Chile's pressing economic problems, the language of Catholic corporatism is likely to ring increasingly hollow, even to the military men and their supporters who seek self-justification for the political-economic line they have chosen. Many of these are sensitive to "world opinion" in any event and, in the absence of international reinforcement, are likely to lose confidence in themselves and in the reasons why they should continue to obey.

CONCLUSIONS

Looking at Chile through the prism of the framework has afforded us a glimpse of several broad "slices" of Chilean history. We moved from a focus of centuries in the discussion of historical-environmental factors; to decades in the treatment of the pre-authoritarian regime; to years and months in the examination of the current domestic and international situations. Each of these foci has provided us with a rather different perspective on the prospects of a successful Chilean transition to authoritarian-corporate rule: although the broadest historical-environmental focus locates important authoritarian trends in the Chilean development process, the examination of pre-authoritarian political institutions and of the domestic and international situations show predominately (though not exclusively) "unfavorable" forces at work. Is there any way that these perspectives can be added up, and if so, what will this tell us about the Chilean future?

It must be emphasized again that it was not the primary purpose of this paper to develop a full-blown explanatory theory or to forecast future developments within Chile itself. The main task, rather, was to inventory the factors felt to contribute to stable authoritarian-corporate rule, to organize these factors within a general framework, and to use this framework as a guide into the complex thicket of Chilean reality. If the framework has indeed shown some useful pathways through these empirical complexities, it can to some extent be considered useful, even if it does not point unambiguously to the way these pathways intersect or to their ultimate destination.

Despite these limitations, however, the framework does contain at least a crude predictive logic which provides at least some clues to the possible outcome in the Chilean case. For the present purpose, the most important aspect of this logic is the assumption, presented in the introduction, that the rubrics under which the individual factors are organized move successively from "distant" to relatively "proximate" causes of a successful authoritarian-corporate transition. Translated into the terms of the Chilean case itself, this means that however "favorable" are the historical legacy and the socioeconomic environment, these factors are not themselves sufficient to consolidate authoritarian-corporate rule. They may do a great deal to explain the breakdown of Chilean "democracy," and they may establish a general "elective affinity" for authoritarian rule; but their greatest impact on this rule is indirect, mediated through pre-authoritarian political institutions and situational pressures and incentives. To the extent that these important mediating factors are not present, historical-environmental factors are not likely to produce a successful transition.[16]

Unfortunately, this does not take us *exceptionally* far in elaborating an unambiguous predictive proposition: at least one important "proximate" factor—the mobilization aspect of the triggering crisis—is present in the Chilean case. As we have seen, this provides a strong incentive for the upper and middle classes to continue to back Chile's current military rulers. In a developmental setting which already contains authoritarian-corporate tendencies, this aspect of the current situation might provide a "springboard" effect through which the junta can complete Chile's institutional transformation. The government's ability to manipulate middle and upper class fears, in other words, might hold opposition from these quarters at bay long enough to implement the government's economic recovery policies. If these policies "take hold," Chile's rulers would then be in a better position to complete the demobilization of the party system and, by drawing on pre-existing bureaucratic patterns, to institutionalize new forms of corporatist rule. To complete the scenario, it is not impossible to imagine that under these conditions the junta could break the vicious circle now precluding high levels of support from the international environment. Domestic stabilization and a toning down of overt repression might well allow the junta to build new bridges to international capital and to status quo oriented Western governments, which in turn would allow a further consolidation of authoritarian-corporate rule at home.

But although one aspect of the triggering crisis does suggest the possibility of a successful transition, the preponderance of pre-authoritarian and situational factors seem to militate against one. Chile's highly mobilized labor opposition, strong centrist and rightist parties, politically unprepared military, severe economic crisis, and unfriendly international environment, all suggest that the current experiment will not take hold and that, in the intermediate future, Chile will be faced with one of two "nonauthoritarian-corporate" political alternatives. One is the development of a more overtly "fascist-totalitarian" system, dominated by an ideologically-oriented mass party which oversees the operation of the government bureaucracy and attempts to mobilize and indoctrinate anti-leftist mass support. A second alternative—one implied in the introduction to this paper—is the "Argentine path" of unstable electoral politics without Marxists.

The "fascist-totalitarian" alternative, while considerably less likely than the other, should nevertheless not be ruled out as a possibility. As evidence of such tendencies, some observers have pointed to the xenophobic and anti-Semitic undertones of the current regime, efforts by the military to penetrate and control broad areas of social life, and the growing visibility of the quasi-fascist Fatherland-and-Liberty movement in the year preceding the overthrow of Allende. An economically disoriented middle class, fearful of the Marxist "enemy," might well be receptive to such developments. And rather than topple the new regime, a highly mobilized labor opposition might well invite (as it already has done in some measure) greater extremes of governmental repression, more extensive efforts at counter-mobilization, and more explicit attempts to elaborate a rightist, anti-Marxist ideology. Such developments might or might not lead to political consolidation, but they would be more along the lines of German fascism than "typical" of authoritarian-corporate regimes.

But Chile lacks some important features of the German archetype. Those who seized power in Chile were not, after all, "marginal men" devoted to a mission of social transformation and supported by a previously mobilized mass following. They were pillars of the established social order—"apolitical" soliders, who are uncomfortable with ideological abstractions and uneasy about the disruptive aspects of mass mobilization. Moreover, even if these leaders were to attempt to construct a fascist movement from the top down, much of the ideological and political space within the rural poor and the urban middle class has already been filled by the established, non-fascist parties of the center and right, as well as by the left itself. Finally, many of the factors which militate against a successful transition to authoritarian-corporate rule work against a facist alternative as well. Chile's severe economic crisis is no more likely to be amenable to a fascist government than to an authoritarian-corporate one; and a fascist regime would be considerably less likely to attract the necessary economic and diplomatic support from the international establishment.

The most likely alternative to authoritarian-corporate rule is thus the restoration of some form of electoral politics. How this restoration will occur—through what mixture of civil-military confrontation and negotiation—remains, of course, to be seen. We know even less about how militaries get out of office than we do about how they get in. But the logic of the preceding analysis does suggest that within some defined period of time, say, three to five years, the military will withdraw, at least temporarily, and that politics in Chile will come to resemble the unsettled electoral competition and praetorian conflict characteristic of her trans-Andean neighbor. On the basis of our previous discussion of Chile's pre-authoritarian and situational factors, I would speculate that the military withdrawal would involve some combination of the following events:

(1) The severity of Chile's economic crisis and the inhospitable international context preclude economic recovery. "Stagflation" continues. Upper and middle class memories of the Allende period fade and there is increasing disaffection with governmental economic programs.

(2) In this context, the apparently moribund center and right parties revive. Never legally disbanded or deprived of their material resources, and with their leadership and communications lines "in place," these parties now begin to hold meetings, issue manifestos, and lend sympathy and support to associated unions and entrepreneurial groups grumbling about tax and credit relief.

(3) At about the same time, many military officers begin to lose confidence in their and the junta's capacity to set Chile's economic house in order. Some advocate a relaxation of the austerity program. Others begin to remember the "apolitical" tradition of the Chilean military in a more favorable light.

(3) Encouraged by cracks in the facade of authoritarian rule, the previously quiescent Chilean left begins to revive. The more moderate

sectors of the Communist and Socialist parties work closely with the Christian Democrats in "stirring up" the union movement. Strikes and confrontations increase. The more radical sectors of the left, meanwhile, begin a wave of kidnapping and terrorism.

(5) The present junta is replaced by a new set of military officers which begins the process of extrication. After bargaining with representatives of the Nationals and the Christian Democrats, a "pact" protecting the "rights" of the military is signed and new elections are scheduled.

(6) A major condition of the pact is that the Communists and Socialists will not be permitted to run candidates and that "subversive" politicians and political movements will be permanently excluded from the political game.

(7) The cycle of unstable "Argentine-style" praetorianism begins.

What does this speculation about Chile's future tell us about the utility of the framework itself? Of course, even if the preceding predictions prove accurate, an enormous amount remains to be done to convert the framework into an explanatory-predictive theory. At a minimum, the "factors" listed under the various rubrics must be converted more explicitly into "variables." That is, the dimensions of such concepts as "dependency" and the degree to which such phenomena can manifest themselves within different countries must be elaborated more clearly than was possible here. Further, the interaction of variables within general categories must be more clearly specified. What is the relative impact of, say, the medieval-Catholic tradition and delayed industrialization in shaping a country's overall pattern of change? What is the relative importance of a mobilized labor force and a cohesive military establishment in determining the ultimate character of the political regime? Finally, the hypothesized relations between variables must be explored in a more general, comparative setting if we are to determine whether "correct" political outcomes in cases such as Chile are predicted for the "right" theoretical reasons.

Notwithstanding its limitations, however, the present analysis does provide at least a step in the direction of theory-building, not only by presenting the conceptual areas from which independent variables may ultimately be elaborated, but also by hazarding guesses about the proximity of these variables to the final outcome. The prediction about Chile which is drawn from the framework thus offers at least some empirical referent by which the framework itself can be evaluated. If the prediction proves wrong and Chile *is* able to consolidate a relatively stable authoritarian-corporate regime, this would quite clearly suggest the need to discard some or all elements of the framework, or to revise the theoretical relationship between them. If, on the other hand, the prediction ventured here does prove correct, this will provide somewhat greater surety that we are asking useful research questions—ones which may allow us to analyze authoritarian-corporate enterprises on something more than an ad hoc, case-by-case basis and which hold out the hope that we may someday be a step ahead of, rather than behind, the events which move forward with such swiftness in the real world.

NOTES

1. Mexico is not generally included as a base of comparison because the "revolutionary" character of its transition seems to set it apart from most other Mediterranean and Latin cases. Given the somewhat uncertain political stability of the other "successful" cases, it may be that the legitimating effect of revolution is a necessary condition for a "fully" institutionalized authoritarian-corporate regime. But this is a proposition which must await exploration elsewhere. On the other hand, although fascist Italy and contemporary Peru are included for some purposes, each is a borderline case. Italy is set apart by its "totalitarian" emphasis on ideology, party rule, and political mobilization, as well as by its cult of leadership and violence. Peru's variant of authoritarian-corporate rule has a populist, "inclusionary" orientation, and its transition is thus in some ways distinct from those of the other, rightist and "exclusionary" regimes (see O'Donnell, 1973: 112). However, the character of the Peruvian military establishment (along with Brazil's) does serve as a useful point of comparison with Chile.

2. Good counter-factual cases are provided by Ongania's Argentina and by Bolivia during the 1960s and 1970s, where efforts to incorporate and control the working class were frustrated in part by resistance from entrenched, broadly-based worker organizations. (see O'Donnell, 1973: 53-201; Malloy, 1970).

3. Rankings are from my own data (Kaufman et al., 1975).

4. Andres Bianchi of CEPAL has been helpful in clarifying for me the impact conservative Catholic University intellectuals on the orientations of the junta (personal communication, 1975).

5. Income data from Valenzuela (1973: 19); growth and inflation data come from A.I.D. (1970).

6. Valenzuela (1972: 75) estimates that in the early 1960s at least 15 percent of the economically active population worked directly for the state and that, even before Allende, the public sector accounted for about 40 percent of the GNP and 58.6 percent of all investments.

7. The figures below show the contrast between Chile (circa 1970) and the other "successful" countries during or after their transition. (Source: Banks, 1971).

	Population in cities of 100,000	Literacy	GDP/Capita	Energy Consumpt./ Capita
Chile	20.6	86.6	645	1113
Portugal	11.7 (1923)	60.0 (1923)	178 (1946)	250 (1949)
Italy	11.9 (1923)	75.7 (1924)	452 (1946)	580 (1948)
Spain	16.7 (1936)	73.5 (1936)	N.A.	610 (1951)
Brazil	20.1 (1964)	57.6 (1964)	271 (1964)	389 (1964)
Peru	21.4 (1968)	66.6 (1968)	243 (1968)	625 (1968)

8. Although social conflict was inextricably linked to the Allende reforms, I do not wish to imply that the breakdown of Chilean constitutionalism itself was necessarily inevitable. My own hunch is that it was not, but this is an issue that must be argued elsewhere.

9. The authors also find that 57 percent of Tomic and Alessandri supporters used ideological terms to explain why they voted *against* Allende. Prothro and Chaparro conclude that "Chilean partisans . . . had clear images of their choices, and those images remained heavily ideological by U.S. standards" (1974: 22).

10. Serious problems of adaptation do, of course, exist for the Marxists. All sectors of the movement must adjust to an underground existence after decades "in the open," an adjustment which requires major changes in leadership style and communications structures. Moreover, serious divisions exist between the Communists and the MIR, which not only constitute the extreme "right" and "left" of the Marxist movement but are also the sectors most capable of switching to underground operations. Each is likely to blame the other for contributing to the collapse of the Allende regime. And although their current predicament pushes them closer together, their disagreement over strategy and tactics remains severe, with the MIR advocating a more radical ("adventuristic and sectarian?") approach and the Communists favoring a more cautious, broad-based ("revisionist?") resistance.

11. By 1969, the military's disgruntlement over deteriorating budgetary support (see Hansen, 1967) combined with mounting political unrest to produce an upswing in military activity. General Roberto Viaux, the leader of a 1969 uprising against the Frei regime, was also an apparent leader of various plots to prevent Allende from taking office. The abortive *tancazo* of June 1973 marked the last stage in the rehearsals which preceded the September 1973 coup.

12. This was the explicit justification given by the armed forces for their intervention (see El Mercurio, 1973).

13. Interestingly, the reason cited in favor of role expansion was not the need for a military "national development" mission, but the need to prepare officers for civilian occupations after they had retired from military duty (Hansen, 1967: 226).

14. Ayres (1973: 510) also finds that 72.6 percent of his sample were willing to grant all groups the right to vote and that "the number willing to deny the vote to Communists was so small that a separate coding category was not established to handle the results."

15. This is not in my judgment the only "lesson" that can be drawn from the Chilean experience. Another plausible one is that the MIR and left-wing Socialist emphasis on the limits of constitutionalism was a self-fulfilling prophecy. Left-wing criticism of Allende's moderation, its opposition to the Communists' call for "consolidation," and its direct action activities, all arguably fostered the escalation and polarization which ultimately led to the collapse of the Allende regime.

REFERENCES

A.I.D. (1970) Summary Economic and Social Indicators for 18 Latin American Countries: 1960-1969. Washington: Office of Development Programs.
ANGELL, A. (1974) "Counter-revolution in Chile." Current History 66, 389 (January).
——— (1972) Politics and the Labour Movement in Chile. London and New York: Oxford Univ. Press.

AYRES, R. L. (1973) "Political history, institutional structure, and prospects for socialism in Chile." Comparative Politics 5, 4 (July).

BANKS, A (1971) Cross-Polity Time-Series Data. Cambridge: M.I.T. Press.

COCKROFT, J., H. RUNDT, and D. JOHNSON (1973) "The multinationals," in D. L. Johnson [ed.] The Chilean Road to Socialism. Garden City: Anchor.

COLLIER, D. (1975) "Timing of economic growth and regime characteristics in Latin America." Comparative Politics 7, 3 (April).

COLLIER, S. (1967) Ideas and Politics of Chilean Independence. London: Cambridge Univ. Press.

CROAN, M. (1970) "Is Mexico the future of East Europe: institutional adaptability and political change in comparative perspective," in S. P. Huntington and C. H. Moore [eds.] Authoritarian Politics in Modern Society, the Dynamics of Established One-Party Systems. New York, London: Basic Books.

CUTRIGHT, P. (1967) "Inequality: a cross-national analysis." Amer. Soc. Rev. 32, 4 (August).

EINAUDI, L. (1973) "Revolution from within?–military rule in Peru since 1968." Studies in Comparative Internal. Develop. 8, 1 (Spring).

El Mercurio (1973) Edicion Internacional Extraordinario (September).

FELIX, D. (1961) "Chile," in A. Pepelasis et al. [eds.] Economic Development, Analysis and Case Studies. New York: Harper.

FLEET, M. H. (1973) "Chile's democratic road to socialism." Western Pol. Q. 27, 4 (December).

FRANK, A. G. (1967) Capitalism and Underdevelopment in Latin America, Historical Case Studies of Chile and Brazil. New York: Monthly Review Press.

GERSCHENKRON, A. (1962) Economic Backwardness in Historical Perspective. Cambridge: Harvard Univ. Press.

GRAHAM, D. H. and T. L. McCOY (1975) "The political-economy of post-Allende Chile: a comparison with Brazil." Delivered at the Annual Meeting of the New England Pol. Sci. Assn. Univ. of Hartford.

HANSEN, R. A. (1967) "Military culture and organizational decline: a study of the Chilean army." Ph.D. dis. Los Angeles: Univ. of California.

HIRSCHMAN, A. O. (1971) "The political economy of import-substituting industrialization in Latin America," in A. O. Hirschman [ed.] A. Bias for Hope. New Haven: Yale Univ. Press.

HOWE, M. (1973) The New York Times (October 23).

HUNTINGTON, S. P. (1968) Political Order in Changing Societies. New Haven: Yale Univ. Press.

JANOS, A. C. (1970) "The one-party state and social mobilization: East Europe between the wars," in S. P. Huntington and C. H. Moore [eds.] Authoritarian Politics in Modern Society: The Dynamics of Established One-Party Systems. New York, London: Basic Books.

JOHNSON, D. L. [ed.] (1973) The Chilean Road to Socialism. Garden City: Anchor.

KAUFMAN, R. R., D. S. GELLER, and H. I. CHERNOTSKY (1975) "A preliminary test of the theory of dependency." Comparative Politics 7, 3 (April).

KAUFMAN, R. R. (1972) The Politics of Chilean Land Reform, 1950-1970. Cambridge: Harvard Univ. Press.

KURTH, J. R. (1973) "Patrimonial authority, delayed development, and Mediterranean politics." Delivered at the Annual Meeting of the Amer. Pol. Sci. Assn., New Orleans.

LANDSBERGER, H. A. (1967) "The labor elite: is it revolutionary?" in S. M. Lipset and A. Solari [eds.] Elites in Latin America. New York: Oxford Univ. Press.
Latin America (1973a) Vol. VII (October 5).
——— (1973b) Vol. VII (October 26).
——— (1973c) Vol. VII (November 9).
——— (1974a) Vol. VII (January 25).
——— (1974b) Vol. VII (February 5).
——— (1974c) Vol. VII (March 15).
LINZ, J. J. (1973) "The future of an authoritarian situation or institutionalization of an authoritarian regime: the case of Brazil," in A. Stepan [ed.] Authoritarian Brazil, Origins, Policies, and Future. New Haven and London: Yale Univ. Press.
——— (1970) "From Falange to movimiento-organizacion: the Spanish single party system and the Franco regime, 1936-1968," in S. P. Huntington and C. H. Moore [eds.] Authoritarian Politics in Modern Society, The Dynamics of Established One-Party Systems. New York, London: Basic Books.
——— (1967) "The party system of Spain: past and future," in S. M. Lipset and S. Rokkan [eds.] Party Systems and Voter Alignments: Cross-National Perspectives. New York and London: Free Press, Collier-MacMillan.
——— (1964) "An authoritarian regime," in E. Allardt and Y. Littunen [eds.] Cleavages, Ideologies and Party Systems. Helsinki: Westermarck Society.
LIPSET, S. M. and S. ROKKAN [eds.] (1967) Party Systems and Voter Alignments: Cross-National Perspectives. New York and London: Free Press, Collier-MacMillan.
LOWENTHAL, A. F. (1974) "Peru's 'revolutionary government of the armed forces': the first five years." Delivered at the Seminar on Continuity and Change in Contemporary Peru. New York.
MALLOY, J. M. (1970) Bolivia: The Uncompleted Revolution. Pittsburgh: Univ. of Pittsburgh Press.
MARX, K. (1959) "The eighteenth brumaire of Louis Bonaparte," in L. S. Feuer [ed.] Basic Writings on Politics and Philosophy, Karl Marx and Friedrich Engels. Garden City: Anchor.
MEDHURST, K. [ed.] (1972) Allende's Chile. London: Hart-Davis MacGibbon.
MENGES, C. (1966) "Public policy and organized business in Chile: a preliminary analysis." J. of Internatl. Affaris, 20, 2.
MORENO, F. J. (1969) Legitimacy and Stability in Latin America, A Study of Chilean Political Culture. New York: New York Univ. Press.
MORSE, R. M. (1973) "The heritage of Latin America," in H. J. Wiarda [ed.] Politics and Social Change in Latin America: The Distinct Tradition. Amherst: Univ. of Massachusetts Press.
MORRIS, J. O. (1966) Elites, Intellectuals, and Consensus. Ithaca: New York State School of Industrial and Labor Relations.
NACLA (1972) New Chile. Berkeley: North America Congress on Latin America.
NEWTON, R. C. (1973) "On 'functional groups,' 'fragmentation,' and 'pluralism,' in Spanish American political society," in H. J. Wiarda [ed.] Politics and Social Change in Latin America: The Distinct Tradition. Amherst: Univ. of Massachusetts Press.
NORTH, L. (1976) "The military in Chilean politics." Studies in Comparative International Develop. 2, 1 (Spring).
NUNN, F. M. (1970) Chilean Politics 1920-1931, The Honorable Mission of the Armed Forces. Albuquerque: Univ. of New Mexico Press.

O'DONNELL, G. A. (1974) "Estado y corporativismo, sobre algunos nuevos aspectos de la dominación política en America Latina." Forthcoming in J. Malloy [ed.] Authoritarianism and Corporatism in Latin America. Pittsburgh: Pittsburgh Univ. Press.
——— (1973) Modernization and Bureaucratic Authoritarianism. Berkeley: Institute of Internatl. Studies.
PAYNE, A. (1968) The Peruvian Coup d'etat of 1962. Washington, D.C. Institute for the Comparative Study of Political Systems.
PETRAS, J. (1973) "Chile: nationalization, socio-economic change and popular participation," in J. Petras and R. LaPorte, Jr. [eds.] Latin America: From Dependence to Revolution. New York, London, Sydney, Toronto: John Wiley.
——— (1969) Politics and Social Forces in Chile. Berkeley: Univ. of California Press.
PIKE, F. B. (1963) Chile and the United States, 1880-1962. Notre Dame: Univ. of Notre Dame Press.
PLASTRIK, S. (1974) "A first word on the Chilean tragedy." Dissent 21, 1 (Winter).
PREGGER, R. C. (1975) "Dependent development in nineteenth century Chile." Ph.D. dis. New Brunswick: Rutgers Univ.
PROTHRO, J. W. and P. E. CHAPARRO (1974) "Public opinion and the movement of Chilean government to the left, 1952-1972." J. of Politics 36, 1 (February).
ROJAS, R. (1973) "The Chilean armed forces: the role of the military in the popular unity government," in D. L. Johnson [ed.] The Chilean Road to Socialism. Garden City: Anchor.
SCHMITTER, P. C. (1974) "Still the century of Corporatism?" Review of Politics 36, 1 (January).
——— (1973) "The Portugalization of Brazil?" in A. Stepan [ed.] Authoritarian Brazil, Origins, Policies, and Future. New Haven and London: Yale Univ. Press.
——— (1972) "Paths to political development in Latin America," in D. A. Chalmers [ed.] Changing Latin America. New York: Academy of Political Science.
——— (1971) Interest Conflict and Political Change in Brazil. Stanford: Stanford Univ. Press.
SIGMUND, P. (1974) "Seeing Allende through the myths." World View 17, 4 (April).
SKIDMORE, T. E. (1967) Politics in Brazil. London, Oxford, New York: Oxford Univ. Press.
STEPAN, A. (1973) "The new professionalism of internal warfare and military role expansion," in A. Stepan [ed.] Authoritarian Brazil, Origins, Policies, and Future. New Haven and London: Yale Univ. Press.
——— (1971) The Military in Politics: Changing Patterns in Brazil. Princeton: Princeton Univ. Press.
SUNKEL, O. (1965) "Change and frustration in Chile," in C. Veliz [ed.] Obstacles to Change in Latin America. London, New York, Toronto: Oxford Univ. Press.
SWEEZY, P. M. (1973) "Chile, the question of power." Monthly Review 25, 7 (December).
TYLER, W. G. and J. P. WOGART (1973) "Economic dependence and marginalization." J. of Interamerican Studies and World Affairs 15, 1 (February).
VALENZUELA, A. (1975) Center-Local Linkages in Chile: Local Government in a Centralized Polity. Durham, N.C.: Duke Univ. Press.
——— (1973) "The breakdown of democracy in Chile." Presented at the Conference on Breakdown and Crises of Democratic Regimes. Yale University.

VALENZUELA, A. (1972) "Political constraints and the prospects for socialism in Chile," in D. A. Chalmers [ed.] Changing Latin America. New York: Academy of Political Science.

WIARDA, H. J. (1973) "Toward a framework for the study of political change in the Iberic-Latin tradition: the corporative model." World Politics 25, 2 (January).